THE WAY OF TRUTH

MATTHEW POLLOCK

This book is set in the typeface *Athelas* designed by Veronika Burian and Jose Scaglione.

Paperback ISBN: 978-1-955546-35-5
Hardcover ISBN: 978-1-088127-40-7

A Publication of *Tall Pine Books*
119 E Center Street, Suite B4A | Warsaw, Indiana 46580
www.tallpinebooks.com

| 1 23 23 20 16 02 |

Published in the United States of America

FOREWORD BY JENTEZEN FRANKLIN

MATTHEW POLLOCK

THE WAY

O

F

TRUTH

"What's right is worth the fight."

"The day we are living in is unique. We have more knowledge at our fingertips than ever, yet fewer people have a firm grasp of the truth. Matthew Pollock talks about that in his book, *The Way of Truth*. Through the powerful words of King David in Psalm 119:30-32, he encourages us all to understand why God's way is the best way. An easy read, *The Way of Truth* invites you on a journey of discerning the times we're in and deciding how you'll approach them. No matter where you find yourself on or off the walk of faith, this book is a must-read!"

PASTOR RUSSELL EVANS
Founder and Senior Pastor, *Planetshakers Church*

"A great book is defined by how many times you want to read it. In his book, *The Way of Truth*, Pastor Matt laid before us a 10-course meal you will want to eat repeatedly. It is not an empty-minded book of shallow thoughts; it is full of delicious divinities. Each of the ten chapters perfectly harmonizes with the others, like mixed spices stirring the appetite. This book will leave you full yet hungry—full of life-changing truths and hungry for more healing and divine adjustments.

When reading *The Way of Truth*, chew on its light, digest its surgeries, and utilize its powers, because once it is loved, the truth breaks chains of deception and heals the perspectives of life. In each chapter, life-giving power is revealed. You will find your rudder reset, your sails opened, your clarity cleansed, your convictions defined, your Rewarder revealed, your heart enlarged, and your hope and faith released."

IVAN TAIT

Speaker and Founder, *What Matters Ministries and Mission*

"In today's culture, many of us are looking for a clear, marked-out path—a black-and-white in a world of gray. While some are seeking their own truth, it's time to return to the reality that there is only one truth. This is what Matthew Pollock unpacks in *The Way of Truth*. Matthew challenges us through Scripture and personal stories to embrace the life-changing principles of God's Word. You'll learn the wisest thing you can do this hour, discuss avoiding detours along your journey, and gain motivation to walk God's path faithfully. Grab a copy for yourself and a friend. You won't want to put this one down!"

PASTOR KEVIN GERALD

Senior Pastor, *Champions Centre*

"Embracing truth is vital to a fulfilling life in Christ. Jesus tells us in John 8:32 that it's what allows us to walk in freedom. Unfortunately, truth has not been as prized in our culture as it once was. Every day, we're living in the reality of ambiguity calling the shots. This is what Matthew passionately and knowledgeably addresses in *The Way of Truth*. Chapter by chapter, he leads us on a journey to the Way, helping us see why God's path is the best path for us and our families. I know you'll be glad you read this book. It's a game-changer!"

PASTOR OBED MARTINEZ
Senior Pastor, *Destiny Church*

"I have known Pastor Matthew for over twenty years and have watched his progress as a pastor of significance in Southern California. I have always thought that he carries so much more than is presently evident and will become a church leader of national prominence.

The Way of Truth reflects his mature insight and prophetic understanding of the church's current dilemma, and it also offers sound biblical solutions. This book is a clarion call for the church to wake up to the hour in which we live. It lays out sobering statistics of the recent decline in church attendance since the COVID-19 pandemic. However, the intent is not to give a sense of despondency but to give hope to contend for the overcoming church that God has promised.

God has already accomplished absolute victory on our behalf, and this book outlines how to defend and walk out that victory. Throughout the pages, the reader is reminded of God's faithfulness to those who prioritize their 'first love,' abandon mediocrity, and long to experience a church in sustained revival.

The best books are interwoven with biblical truth but also with personal challenges and triumphs. Pastor Matthew describes such a challenge as an 'Abraham moment' in his life. I was particularly touched by his story of sacrifice and the subsequent reward that follows, and I am sure it will encourage every reader.

Pastor Matthew confirms to those seeking God's supernatural presence daily that we are on the cusp of a great outpouring of unprecedented power that ancient prophets only caught a glimpse of in their time. *The Way of Truth* is an inspirational call to know the master plan for God's church in these turbulent times, and it outlines His strategy. If you are passionate about the future of the church and God's plans, this book is for you. Enjoy!"

PASTOR TOM INGLIS

Psalmody International

"Our world is so fast-paced. Every minute of every day, mixed messages fly at us from various directions. With so many opinions, how do we know what's true? That's what Matthew Pollock addresses in *The Way of Truth*. He outlines what God calls truth and what embracing this truth can mean to our lives. He encourages us that we're on the verge of a revival in America, but it likely won't come through political reform. It will come from you and me making a firm decision that, as for us and our homes, we will serve the Lord. I am confident—if you let it, this book will change your life!"

PHILIP L. LIBERATORE

CPA, IRS Problem Solver & Ordained Minister

DEDICATION

To the ones God has given me:

*Abby—my beloved wife, your loving,
dedicated support is invaluable.*

*Talon, Kaleb, Hope, and Brooke—you make being
a father the greatest pleasure.*

I am so grateful to walk this journey with you—to the end.

*"I have chosen **the way of truth**;*

Your judgments I have laid before me.

I cling to Your testimonies;

O Lord, do not put me to shame!

I will run the course of Your commandments,

For You shall enlarge my heart."

PSALM 119:30-32

ACKNOWLEDGEMENTS

To The Way Family Church: This day! This day! This people! Thank you for being an amazing group—sincere, devoted, faithful, and God-fearing. It has been an incredible honor for Abby and me to pastor you these past 14 years. To the end!

To my parents, Greg and Janet Pollock: Thank you for everything! Your constant and continual love, support, and partnership are priceless. I am honored to be your son and to have been raised by you in the most amazing, godly way. You're the best!

To Troy and April Pollock: What a team! I sincerely thank you for being so instrumental in this endeavor and so committed to its fulfillment.

To Dan and Rosanne Gallegos: I love, value, and appreciate you so much. You matter!

To Dana and Tammie Stevenson: Great is your reward! Your lives, partnership, and support all these years have served as a continual gift and source of great strength.

To Martin and Ale Topete: Better together! God knows how you and your family's dedication and faithfulness have served as an incredible blessing for all!

To our staff and team: What an honor it is to serve with you! Abby and I love you and are forever grateful to walk alongside you.

CONTENTS

FOREWORD

WHEN ONLY ONE in three returned to church following the pandemic, churches nationwide and even worldwide felt the effects of the months when our houses of worship fell silent. Church did not stop, thanks to technology, but a change was in the air. The aftereffects of the shutdowns changed the landscape of "church" in America, and many churches did not survive the impact.

The Way of Truth by Matthew Pollock uses research to paint the picture of the post-pandemic church and its challenges while revealing solutions found in Scripture, showing the roadmap to victory. While research points to a pivot away from the disciplines of the faith: church attendance, tithing, and studying God's Word, it also paints the picture of a nation more desperate for the power of the local church than ever before.

The moral decline of the world's nations is as great or greater than at any time in history, with continued devastating results. There is so much to learn about the effects of COVID-19, the shutdowns, and the fallout of political and religious division. Matthew Pollock has gone to great lengths to paint an accurate and detailed picture of the church's influence through solutions found in the Bible. His book will inform you, arm you with facts, and infuse you with the truths found in Scripture that transcend the circumstances of the day the way they have for centuries.

As you read each page, it will become apparent that the church has been here many times. We were here every time God's people were led off into captivity in the Old Testament, and we were here while under Roman oppression in the days when Jesus walked the earth. Every time the world has tried to count the church out, our greatest victories shifted the trajectory of history, and our greatest revivals took the stage.

The Way of Truth is filled with facts for the hour we are in, but it is ultimately filled with hope, promise, and a plan authored by the Creator of the world and handed down through the ages echoing the most comforting words you could hear: "We win." When all is said and done, *every* knee will bow, and *every* tongue will confess that Jesus Christ is Lord. On THAT day, we will all declare with one voice—we won.

Be a light to your world. You have a role to play, and your family is in the enemy's crosshairs. Do not shrink back. Do not walk in fear and intimidation. Instead, walk in victory and with an uncommon confidence in even the most desperate of times, because you walk in the Way of Truth.

JENTEZEN FRANKLIN
Senior Pastor, *Free Chapel*
New York Times Best-Selling Author

INTRODUCTION

UPON FINISHING BIBLE school, I naively thought a pastorate would fall into my lap. So, when that didn't happen, it forced me to embrace a season I hadn't expected. My wife, Abby, and I took "regular" jobs while we trusted God for the right door to open. Abby waited tables, and I worked as a courier.

We made many wonderful memories during that time. Still, throughout our season of waiting, I often struggled with striving. I wanted to fulfill the call of God so badly that for a while, I tried hard to make things happen on my own. When my ambition tripped me up, God was always faithful to help me get back to a place of trust.

One of the most memorable of these times happened when our oldest son, Talon, was only three years old. Abby was waiting tables that evening, so I took him to an event at the church we were attending. It was a gathering of pastors and leaders, and my main reason for being there was honestly to make some connections.

Talon had other plans, though. As the night service ended, he grew cranky. No matter what I did, I couldn't calm him down. Finally, frustrated and upset, I left the service to take Talon to my parent's house, where we were living. I wanted to tuck him into bed quickly so that I could return to the church in time for the meet-and-greet.

On my way to take Talon to sleep, I realized he hadn't had dinner yet, so I grabbed a banana. When I reached out to hand it to him, the Spirit of God spoke to me and said, "Matthew, *never* neglect the ones I have given you."

It's hard to explain the holy sense of conviction I felt at that moment. Though I was set on fulfilling God's call on my life, I realized I was trying to do it *my* way. So, this time, I ran downstairs and grabbed another banana for myself. I laid down by Talon as I unpeeled it and said, "You know what, buddy? Who cares about tonight? This is my world. *You're* my world." We enjoyed that change of plans for the rest of the night.

My plans weren't the only thing that changed, though. My perspective changed, too. So did my priorities, not to mention my *life*. The next morning, I wrote the Holy Spirit's profound words at the top of my Bible, and in every Bible I've owned since then.

Never neglect the ones I have given you.

It's my mantra, my mission, and my purpose, and it has been so for over two decades. As I have focused on the ones God has given me, He has taken care of everything else. He has made and continues to make the dreams He placed in my heart a reality. One of those dreams is this book. It has been in my heart to write this for years, but at the start of 2022, I knew it was time to begin. Thankfully, God gave me the most beautiful confirmation to spur me on.

At the start of every year, our church holds 21 days of prayer. Our church family anonymously writes what we are believing for on prayer cards. Then, for three weeks, we gather and agree with each other daily in prayer. One day after a gathering, I casually mentioned to our youngest, Brooke, that I was finally writing this book. I'll never forget the look on her face.

"Well, Dad. I need something new for my prayer card," she smiled. "My prayer for the last three years has been answered."

This book truly is an answered prayer for my family and me, and my greatest hope is that it becomes the same for you. I'm so glad you're here, and I'm looking forward to embarking on this journey together. *Finally.* Now, let's get started.

CHAPTER ONE

AS FOR ME AND MY HOUSE

DEEP IN THE heart of every person lies the yearning for one thing. It's an answer to a question that humankind has asked for all of time. This question has been found on the lips of innocent children with developing minds, and on the tongues of our world's brightest philosophers. We find it hidden in ancient documents and contemporary song lyrics. We hear it asked in various forms at dinner tables, in conference rooms, and on the evening news.

This question burned deeply in the heart of one historical figure with a world-changing decision to make. It was the greatest hour of human history, and he was the man in charge. His name was Pontius Pilate.

Pontius Pilate was the fifth governor of Judea who served under the Roman emperor. The emperor tasked Pilate with overseeing the trial of a Jew who had caused quite a stir among the locals. They called Him Jesus. He had grown up among them, raised in the small town of Nazareth. Jesus claimed to be the Messiah, and some who followed Him believed that claim. Others considered it blasphemy.

Once every year, the Roman courts allowed one prisoner to be freed. Pilate was to decide if this prisoner would be Jesus, or if it would be Barabbas, a criminal. John 18 gives us the account of the trial. Verses 33 through 38 say:

> Then Pilate entered the Praetorium again, called Jesus, and said to Him, "Are You the King of the Jews?" Jesus answered him, "Are you speaking for yourself about this, or did others tell you this concerning Me?" Pilate answered, "Am I a Jew? Your own nation and the chief priests have delivered You to me. What have You done?" Jesus answered, "My kingdom is not of this world. If My kingdom were of this world, My servants would fight, so that I should not be delivered to the Jews; but now My kingdom is not from here." Pilate therefore said to Him, "Are You a king then?" Jesus answered, "You say rightly that I am a king. For this cause I was born, and for this

cause I have come into the world, that I should bear witness to the truth. Everyone who is of the truth hears My voice." Pilate said to Him, "What is truth?"...

What is truth?

There it is—the age-old question every person has sought an answer to. Why? Because deep down, we understand this reality: Truth is the only foundation upon which success can be built. A successful society. A successful relationship. A successful verdict. A successful *anything*. Truth is the anchor that sustains the soul from the tremors, tribulations, and traumas of life. It is the footing every person needs to make progress, overcome obstacles, and look past disappointment in the hope of a better tomorrow.

This is largely because truth generates trust, and nothing grows healthily without trust. It's why, in the American court of law, every witness must commit to truth. They must affirm that they will testify honestly because the court acknowledges that without truth, there's no justice. There's only chaos—a word I believe most of us would deem appropriate to describe our culture today.

> "Truth is the anchor that sustains the soul from the tremors, tribulations, and traumas of life."

In a recent survey by Deseret News' *Faith in America*,

between 1995 and 2021, the number of Americans who identified as religious "nones" (having no religious beliefs) climbed from 6 percent to 21 percent, as reported by Gallup researchers.[1] Today, 43% of millennials "don't know, care, or believe that God exists."[2] These realities scream of a people desperately asking the same question Pontius Pilate uttered that day. The good news is that Pilate found the answer, and we can find it, too. John 18:38-19:5 gives more of the story. The passage says:

... And when he had said this, he went out again to the Jews, and said to them, "I find no fault in Him at all. But you have a custom that I should release someone to you at the Passover. Do you therefore want me to release to you the King of the Jews?" Then they all cried again, saying, "Not this Man, but Barabbas!" Now Barabbas was a robber. So then Pilate took Jesus and scourged Him. And the soldiers twisted a crown of thorns and put it on His head, and they put on Him a purple robe. Then they said, "Hail, King of the Jews!" And they struck Him with their hands. Pilate then went out again, and said to them, "Behold, I am bringing Him out to you, that you may know that I find no fault in Him." Then Jesus came out, wearing the crown of thorns and the purple robe. And Pilate said to them, "Behold the Man!"

BEHOLD THE MAN

These last three words—"Behold the Man"—prove Pilate's revelation that the truth is a man, and He is Jesus.

God has "behold" moments, like Pilate's, for all of us. As a pastor, one privilege of my life is witnessing them. I treasure the times I get to watch as a person's eyes open and their hearts soften to the message of John 14:6— that Jesus Christ is the way, the truth, and the life.

That's because this one fact changes the game. It shifts everything when we realize that every system and structure of the world is tainted with lies, making it faulty. But Jesus? Lying is impossible for Him, making Him completely faithful. Everything outside of Him is error; everything inside of Him is perfect.

Now, if you think deeply as I do, while this may encourage you, you may also still have some questions about how we can be *sure* Jesus is the truth. There are two ways I know, and two ways I believe you can, too. The first is based on numbers. The Old Testament is full of messianic prophecies that foretold exactly what would occur when the Messiah came to earth. Mathematician Peter Stoner concluded that the probability of one man fulfilling just 48 of the messianic prophecies is 1 in 10^{157}. That's 10 with 157 zeros

> "Everything outside of Him is error; everything inside of Him is perfect."

after it! But Jesus did not only fulfill 48 prophecies; He fulfilled all 324 prophecies *exactly* as they were written.[3] That is not a coincidence. That is *proof*.

The second way we know Jesus is the truth isn't based on numbers; it comes from what Pilate experienced: personal revelation. It's the supernatural knowledge he received as he watched a sinless man beaten to death for the sins of those who had rejected, scourged, and crucified Him. The word *behold* means to stand in awe and be amazed. So when Pilate said, "Behold the man," with wonder and reverence, he recognized the truth of who Jesus was and is—the answer to every heart's deepest question.

While you read this book, my heartfelt prayer is that if you haven't yet, you experience a *behold* moment. When we receive the revelation that we have the incredible privilege to *know* the truth—to serve, follow, love, and be loved by Him—this sets us on the path to calm the chaos in our lives, families, communities, nation, and world. When we walk in the way of truth, we willingly and wholeheartedly pledge our loyalty to Jesus— the Man. The one who cannot fail. The stability of our times, and the anchor for our days. Jesus alone is the rock of ages, and our solid ground in every season.

As we embark on the journey of this book together, we'll touch on many attacks on truth present in our culture today. Some you may be aware of; some you may not. Either way, I encourage you to look at each one with fresh eyes and an open heart. There are many I deal with daily as a pastor, but two stand out in this hour: the decline in honor for spiritual disciplines and a lacking pulpit.

KEEP IT HOLY

We learned about it in Sunday school—in the ten commandments given to Moses, commandment number five is, "Remember the Sabbath day and keep it holy." But in what many call "Post-Christian America," it's hard to imagine a time when Sunday's streets were littered with closed shops and restaurants as we set aside the Sabbath for church and rest.

It has taken generations, but honor for God's day seems to have dwindled dramatically. Instead of using it for His purpose, we work, play sports, sleep in, or prepare for the week ahead. I understand some people can't choose whether they work on Sunday, but my point is that things have changed. Most Christian Americans now do everything but honor God's original design for the day. And when COVID-19 turned our lives upside down in 2020, it seemed to push what little respect our culture had left for the Sabbath out the window.

During the lockdowns, technology offered the wonderful alternative of streaming services, but the online option was never meant to be a permanent substitute. And the virus was never a valid excuse to avoid attending church altogether. Barna Research Group studied church attendance for the first four months of lockdowns, and their findings were surprising. They discovered that 32% of practicing Christians who typically attend church at least monthly reported not streaming an online service during that time.[4] I'd venture to say that number has only increased.

A few months later, the same research group found that only one in three practicing Christians returned to their pre-COVID-19 local church, attending there exclusively. However, it does not imply that most switched churches; 32% of practicing Christians stopped attending altogether.[5]

It's not just about Sundays, though. It seems we have also lost our honor for tithing, praying, and studying God's Word. In one of America's most pivotal hours in history, spiritual discipline has been found lacking. This didn't just happen; it's been in the works for generations. We gradually chose one compromise here and there until our moral decline reached a place of significance. That individual decline affected our families, our families affected our communities, and our communities affected our nation.

> "God wants us to do things His way, and they work out best when we do."

The biblical principle will always be true: slacking on godly disciplines causes things to go awry. But when we uphold God's standards, everything else falls into place. One of the best examples of this is Chick-Fil-A, which is famously closed on Sundays. The website says this about their countercultural decision:

> Our founder, Truett Cathy, decided to close on Sundays in 1946 when he opened his first restaurant in Hapeville, Georgia. Having worked seven

days a week in restaurants open 24 hours, Truett saw the importance of closing on Sundays so that he and his employees could set aside one day to rest and worship if they choose—a practice we uphold today.[6]

According to *Business Insider*, Chick-fil-A likely loses more than $1 billion a year because of this decision[7], but it gains much more. With their average sales per store, not including mall locations reaching approximately $7.1 million in 2020, Chick-Fil-A generates more sales per store than any large fast-food restaurant in the United States—even the 24/7 ones.[8] It proves the universal reality: God wants us to do things His way, and they work out best when we do.

A LACKING PULPIT

Another alarming actuality is the obvious moral decline not just of the general Christian population but of those leading it, too. I am a pastor, so I understand the unique pressures pastors are constantly under, naturally and spiritually. In the good and the hard, I always cheer on these heroes, aware that we all sin and fall short of God's glory.

With that said, my heart genuinely breaks with deep sorrow and compassion every time I hear of another leadership scandal or pastor falling. It reminds me that we are neither excluded from the enemy's schemes nor immune to the temptations he offers. Most pastors and leaders I know have solid integrity and are leading strong, healthy churches. But because of sin's work in the world, unfortunately, some have not chosen well. The result has affected both those sitting in front of the pulpit and those standing in it.

I'm sure there are several reasons for this decline, but with a humble heart, I suggest one to you: a lacking pulpit. Probably unknowingly, many of us pastors, at one time or another, have approached the pulpit with a deficiency of truth, and I believe this has contributed to many of society's problems.

If you are familiar with church and culture, it's not hard to see how we've made this mistake. For one, many pastors, though pure-hearted, have not engaged in the depth of study necessary to adequately teach God's Word. (In our defense, with the increasing demands of pastoral ministry and decreasing tithe to pay more staff, we may not have been given the time.) As a result, Scripture is not put into full context, and our congregations don't receive all God wants them to hear.

Another reason is that many churches have shifted from presence sensitivity to people sensitivity. Our hearts have likely been honorable in wanting to attract more people to the gospel, but to cater to the attendee, God's Word has become watered down. Doing so allows people to settle into their environment instead of challenging them to change it. In my opinion, this is when some churches started feeling more like a producer-consumer relationship and less like a church family. But here's the truth: it will never be jokes or politically correct speeches that transform us; it will always be God's holy, sacred Word.

Now, before you assume you were born into humanity's most troubling hour, let me clarify something. It's easy to get lost in these realities, assuming our times are unique, but it has always been this way. There have always been periods when God's people honored Him well, and others in which they rebelled.

From the Old Testament to the New Testament, we continually see variations of God reminding His people to keep Him first. Moses translated God's words into a commandment: "You shall have no other gods before Me" (Exodus 20:3 ESV). Paul describes God as having preeminence in all things (Colossians 1:18). God has never changed His mind. He must *always* and *only* be first.

> "It will never be jokes or politically correct speeches that transform us; it will always be God's holy, sacred word."

LETTERS TO THE CHURCHES

Throughout Scripture, God sometimes forewarns about the future while also describing the present. In Revelation 2 and 3, we read about a vision given to John during his exile on the island called Patmos. In this vision, Jesus reads seven letters—one to each of the churches in Asia Minor, which is present-day Turkey. The letters address what was happening in the church of the day while also predicting what would later happen.

These writings give us indispensable wisdom. They make God's measuring stick of judgment clear, proving what He honors and rejects. Sadly, most churches got rejected, with only two receiving a blessing and five receiving a rebuke. Many have *always* been called; few have *always* been chosen. As we read His judgments of Ephesus, Smyrna, Pergamos, Thyatira, Sardis, Philadelphia, and Laodicea, we will probably see a bit of ourselves in each one.

Ephesus was a church of 30,000. Young Timothy, the Apostle Paul's protégé, was the pastor. Full of fear, he cut his teeth in this atmosphere—preaching to a large, powerful megachurch. This church had lost its first love, and as a result, they were not living His way. Today, Ephesus would be the large church down the street with a big bank account, notoriety, and the best sound and lighting systems. It would be filled with blue-collar hard workers who are gifted, educated, and up-to-date on political happenings. This church would look like they have it all together but would fail to keep Jesus' two prime commandments—loving God and loving your neighbor.

Smyrna was one of the two churches not rebuked. You likely wouldn't be lining up outside this church's door, though. It was radical, and as a result, many in the church endured persecution, hardship, and even martyrdom. Through it all, Smyrna remained faithful to the end.

Pergamos breaks your heart. This church looked just like the world. They were a people of complete compromise, allowing idols, immorality, cults, and heresy among them. They had a Burger King "have-it-your-way" vibe, refusing to deny Christ, but accepting other gods, too.

Thyatira was the church that allowed false prophets and false teachings. They welcomed wrong doctrine, idolatry, sexual sin, and pagan traditions. Their strengths were love, faith, and good works, and Jesus complimented that. Unfortunately, the bad choked out the good.

Sardis was the spiritually dead church. Jesus basically told them, "You think you're alive, but you're dead." Talk about a wake-up call! This church had declined in its faith to the point that they were going through the motions. They had fallen asleep to the things of Jesus.

Philadelphia was the second of the two churches commended. I believe this church should be an example for us to follow. Philadelphia started and ended well, and Jesus promised to protect them from trouble because of their faithfulness.

In my opinion, the last church—Laodicea—characterizes the American church today. Once strong and on fire for God, this church had fallen into the middle ground of lukewarm indifference. They were halfway in and halfway out. They went through the motions of living for God when it was convenient, but they relied on their riches more than they relied on God. This church received nothing but rebuke.

The sad part is that this church thought they were doing okay. But Jesus said, "I know your deeds, that you are neither cold nor hot. I wish you were either one or the other! So, because you are lukewarm—neither hot nor cold—I am about to spit you out of my mouth" (Revelation 3:15-16 NIV).

With this statement, Jesus made it clear—He *hates* mediocrity.

TO HIM WHO OVERCOMES

I know this all feels heavy but be encouraged—it doesn't end like this. Throughout the letters, Jesus gives us great hope with the repetitive use of one phrase. He made this statement to every single church, whether they were rebuked or commended. Read through the passage, and you'll find it: "To him who overcomes." In God's goodness, He also leaves them with a promise after He judges each of the seven churches. He leaves *us* with a promise. *Victory*.

Jesus never promised this faith walk would be easy. He warns us that there will be much warfare along the path. Everyone will experience pain and trauma. That's just life in a fallen, corrupt world. Believers go through what the world goes through; we just go through it differently. This helps us choose confidence in even the most troubling times because we know it's a fixed fight. The cross of Calvary has already decided and defeated everything we'll ever face. The battles will always come, but we can overcome them because Jesus overcame death.

Jesus says, "I have told you these things, so that in me you may have peace. In this world you will have trouble. But take heart! I have overcome the world" (John 16:33). If you break down the word used for *overcome* in these letters, it is the Greek word *nikáō*, which means "to overcome, conquer, be victorious."[9] (Yes—it's where they got the brand name Nike from.)

No matter where you are today, Jesus promises you *can* overcome! You can be victorious. This is why you should always be of good cheer, despite the statistics. It's why you should always sing, though some days you might feel overwhelmed. It is also why you should never let the state of our culture cause your faith to waver. The enemy had a plan, but the blood of Jesus intercepted it. He is the victor's crown, and He holds the victory for everyone who calls on His name. "Many *are* the afflictions of the righteous, but the Lord delivers him out of them all" (Psalm 34:19).

The victory is there for you, but you have a part to play in receiving it. You've got to agree with it, protect it, and walk it out daily. When we agree with victory, we respond to negative circumstances differently. We don't respond with worry or stress but with joy. We act like Paul, who said, "That is why, for Christ's sake, I delight in weaknesses, in insults, in hardships, in persecutions, in difficulties. For when I am weak, then I am strong" (2 Corinthians 12:10 NIV).

It's vital to put the Word of the Lord upon our mouths, rise in our homes and declare that our families are strong. Our churches are strong. I don't care what it looks like—don't diminish your message. Declare the Word of the Lord!

In addition to agreeing with victory, we also have to protect it. We see this example throughout Scripture—people defending their right to victory, vigilantly protecting their ground. In Genesis 15, as Abraham offers a sacrifice in covenant with God, the ravens wait to take it. That's how the enemy is. He's always waiting on the sidelines, ready to snatch away what God intends to give. God's gift of victory is available to you, but it's not guaranteed. So, protect His victory over your mind, marriage, family, and life. Shoo off the ravens and defend it.

After we agree with and defend our victory, we must walk it out. We've got to remind ourselves as often as necessary that we are new creatures. The old has passed away. When we fail, we can repent and get back on track. Because of God's goodness, in every season, in every way, we *can* overcome—in our lives, families, churches, communities, and nations.

WHAT THE LOCUST HAS EATEN

Earlier, we mentioned some sobering statistics, but my heart is that you see them through this hopeful lens: though they are facts, I believe they won't be final. Yes, the enemy has stolen much in our lives, churches, communities, and nation, but as Paul says in Ephesians 4:28, "Let him who stole steal no longer...." It's time for a restoration of righteousness resulting in God's healing touch!

We find one of the most encouraging biblical stories of restoration in the book of Joel. It was written to the people of Judah between 830 and 800 BC. Joel, a prophet of the Israelites' Southern Kingdom, penned this 73-verse book as a poem. It contains 50 clear commandments regarding how the people should live amid "the day of the Lord"—the day Jesus returns.

The word of the LORD that came to Joel son of Pethuel. Hear this, you elders; listen, all who live in the land. Has anything like this ever happened in your days or in the days of your ancestors? Tell it to your children, and let your children tell it to their children, and their children to the next generation. What the locust swarm has left the great locusts have eaten; what the great locusts have left the young locusts have eaten; what the young locusts have left other locusts have eaten (Joel 1:1-4 NIV).

Four types of locusts devastated Judah and Jerusalem. Joel called them the chewing locust, the swarming locust, the crawling locust, and the consuming locust. The land was left leveled, and the fields of grain, vineyards, gardens, and trees were completely bare. As a result, a severe famine swept throughout the land. In this dark hour, Joel warned Judah, using the locusts as a symbol of the enemy and the devastation he wanted to bring to them. The Israelites' sin had become so great that they had opened the door wide to God's divine judgment. But then, as He always does, God offered a promise, a "to him who overcomes" moment.

"'Yet even now,' declares the Lord, 'return to me with all your heart, with fasting, with weeping, and with mourning; and rend your hearts and not your garments.' Return to the Lord your God, for he is gracious and merciful, slow to anger, and abounding in steadfast love; and he relents over disaster" (Joel 2:12-13 ESV).

God told the people that they still had a choice. If they chose not to repent, enemy armies would devour the land. However, if they humbled themselves, fasted, prayed, and sought His face, He would renew their supply and fully restore them. He promised, "I will repay you for the years the locusts have eaten—And afterward, I will pour out my Spirit on all people. Your sons and daughters will prophesy, your old men will dream dreams, your young men will see visions" (Joel 2:25, 28 NIV).

We're living in the day of the locust again. Not physically but metaphorically, as we see our nation ravaged by sin, its moral fabric ripped apart. Thankfully, as Hebrews 13:8 says, God is the same yesterday, today, and forever. He wants to restore what the locust has eaten in your life, marriage, and family. He wants to restore what the locust has eaten in our churches, communities, and nation. But as in Judah's day, it's our choice, and the right choice remains the same: repent. Don't live a lukewarm life. Return to your first love. Then, and *only* then, you will experience true, abundant restoration.

I'm no end-time expert, but based on biblical evidence, I believe we are approaching "the day of the Lord." It's more important than ever to discern the hour. As the days grow more intense, we've got to seek God incessantly. We've got to follow His Word more closely, resist temptation more fully, and lead our families more vigilantly. We must use our time well and not give our energy to lesser things because we need the strength to answer when God calls.

Now is not the time to stop gathering as the body of Christ, studying God's Word, or tithing to the local church. It's time to take spiritual disciplines seriously. Now is not the time to delegate our children to the school systems; it's time to rise and steward them well. It's time to make a dedicated decision to choose God's way.

Even in the anti-Christ pollution of our age, God is

still good. And He always will be. He wants to heal, restore and refresh our land, pouring out His Spirit afresh.

I don't know where you are today. Maybe you relate to the church of Ephesus. You've gotten caught up in power, money, or notoriety. Maybe you're like Pergamos. You've compromised. Maybe you're like Thyatira, and you've strayed. Maybe, like Sardis, you've fallen asleep. Or maybe, like Laodicea, you've lost your first love. Wherever you are, you can rejoice in this truth: victory is in your blood. You can overcome and see your life restored. But *you* have to choose.

> "It's time to make a dedicated decision to choose God's way."

We can't deny that what we've lost is precious. But what is in front of us is even more so. So, what will you decide? I have decided. As for me and my house, we will serve the Lord.

CHAPTER TWO

SIGNS AND SOLUTIONS

IN THE LAST chapter, we focused on the natural realities of the hour we live in, shared statistics on culture, and grew excited about where we can go from here. Perhaps many of us even made a renewed decision to walk and lead our families in God's way—the Way of Truth. In this chapter, we'll concentrate on getting from where we are to that road to victory.

To experience victory in anything, we must first discern what we will encounter. So, to begin, let's converge on what's happening beyond what we can see. "For we do not wrestle against flesh and blood, but against principalities, against powers, against the rulers of the darkness of this age, against spiritual *hosts* of wickedness in the heavenly places" (Ephesians 6:12). The Apostle Paul is saying that we're not fighting a person or place, politician, or party. We're not only fighting through sickness, depression, or anxiety but more is happening in the unseen world. We're fighting Satan and his forces of evil.

Satan knows we're living in biblical times. It's not a theory for discussion or debate; it's a fact according to Scripture. He knows believers are the restraining force keeping him from taking over the earth. He's aware that his time is short, so he's turning up the heat, working overtime to oppose us.

The Bible predicted this would be the case, presenting the challenging nature of our day. But thank God, He gave us a way to prevail now and in eternity. He offers two things in Scripture that help us handle this season well. First, He gives us *signs* to confirm that we live in what many call the "end times." Then, He gives us *solutions* that help us live with an eternal kingdom mindset, prevailing through every pressure.

That's what I love most about God. Foremost, He is our Father, but not just any father. Our Father is the greatest of all time. Throughout Scripture, we see that, like any good father, God's utmost concern is His children. He wants to ensure our protection, security, provision, and restoration. That's why He gives us signs of Jesus' impending return and solutions to live well while we're waiting.

Let's look at some signs. Though you may have read

these, I encourage you not to skip past or skim through them. Instead, read them closely, intentionally noting attitudes and realities prevalent today.

> But know this, that in the last days perilous times will come: For men will be lovers of themselves, lovers of money, boasters, proud, blasphemers, disobedient to parents, unthankful, unholy, unloving, unforgiving, slanderers, without self-control, brutal, despisers of good, traitors, headstrong, haughty, lovers of pleasure rather than lovers of God, having a form of godliness but denying its power. And from such people turn away! For of this sort are those who creep into households and make captives of gullible women loaded down with sins, led away by various lusts, always learning and never able to come to the knowledge of the truth (2 Timothy 3:1-7).

This passage is chock-full of current struggles, but every time I read it, the last one stands out to me. It says, "always learning and never able to come to the knowledge of the truth." In a time when technology offers the greatest worship music and messages with one click, are we *really* making progress in our faith? Jesus declared a sign of the coming times: "And then many will be offended, will betray one another, and will hate one another. Then many false prophets will rise up and deceive many. And because lawlessness will abound, the love of many will grow cold. But he who endures to the end shall be saved" (Matthew 24:10-13).

These verses express reasons why many do not progress in their faith—offense, betrayal, false teaching, and the Laodicea-like problems of lukewarm Christianity and a replaced first love. But there's one phrase that seems to sum up the day in which we are living. Jesus declared, "...because lawlessness will abound, the love of many will grow cold." He's predicting today's massive exposure to and expansion of evil.

It's not something that has happened by chance; it is a strategic ploy of the enemy. Society has become so inundated with evil that it has grown desensitized to it, causing many hearts to grow cold to the things of God. These are just a few of the signs God gives us in Scripture. Now, let's look at the solution.

> But the day of the Lord will come as a thief in the night, in which the heavens will pass away with a great noise, and the elements will melt with fervent heat; both the earth and the works that are in it will be burned up. Therefore, since all these things will be dissolved, what manner of persons ought you to be in holy conduct and godliness, looking for and hastening the coming of the day of God, because of which the heavens will be dissolved, being on fire, and the elements will melt with fervent heat? Nevertheless we, according

to His promise, look for new heavens and a new earth in which righteousness dwells. Therefore, beloved, looking forward to these things, be diligent to be found by Him in peace, without spot and blameless; and consider that the longsuffering of our Lord is salvation..." (2 Peter 3:10-1).

In this passage, Peter speaks of "the day of the Lord"—the day of God's final judgment, when He will settle the earth's injustices once and for all. It will be both a great and terrible day—great for those who received salvation and terrible for those who did not. In this passage, we're urged to live prepared and pleasing to God in eager anticipation of Jesus' coming.

Another New Testament passage that offers solutions is Luke 22:31-32. Here, Jesus tells Peter (also called Simon), "Simon, Simon! Indeed, Satan has asked for you, that he may sift *you* as wheat. But I have prayed for you, that your faith should not fail; and when you have returned to *Me,* strengthen your brethren." This passage might be short, but it is full of insight. In these two verses, Jesus conveys three things we must discern about our day—it's serious, it's specific, and it's spiritual.

IT'S SERIOUS

There's no refuting the tone with which Jesus addresses Peter. It's serious. He's giving him kingdom perspective, urging him to push off naivety and distraction and recognize the intention and attack of the enemy. God uses this same tone throughout the Old and New Testaments, utilizing parallels of the end times to highlight the urgency of our day.

We find one parallel in the story of Noah. In Hebrews 11:7, we're told, "By faith Noah, being divinely warned of things not yet seen, moved with godly fear, prepared an ark for the saving of his household, by which he condemned the world and became heir of the righteousness which is according to faith." Here, God tells us to live seriously because it's a day for *godly fear.*

Joel 2:11 calls the day Jesus will return "the great and terrible day of the Lord." Here, we're warned: live seriously because it's a day of *judgment.* Then, another parallel in the book of Joel is mentioned in the last chapter. This one is encouraging. Here, God shows us: live seriously, for today is the day of *repentance*—repentance that leads to restoration.

Amidst all these things that *today* is for, I will add a few more based on Scripture. Today is a day of action. It's a day to ensure those in your relational circles have found hope. It's a time for church, prayer, and the right priorities. It's a time to prioritize Jesus and His kingdom and, as Paul writes, to make *Him* preeminent (Colossians 1:18).

It's not time to walk out on your marriage or children; it's time to steward what God has given you well. It's not time to be casual with Christianity; it's time to press forward. It's not time to get lazy about spiritual disciplines; it's time to push past apathy. It's not time to live isolated; it's time to create community. It's not time to walk around defeated; it's time to hold on to hope, trusting in the One who brought victory. It's time to live undistracted by other peoples' paths, focusing on what God has called *you* to do. It's time to be still, follow grace, and discern your relationships. It's time to live seriously.

I understand this is a sober admonishing, but take heart! Though we must be serious about today, we can live in deep, overflowing joy. We can be grateful that even in the most troubling times, we have the most extraordinary defender in God. He will be our shelter for today and our salvation for tomorrow.

IT'S SPECIFIC

The second thing Jesus shows through His conversation with Peter is that our times are specific. Just as Jesus called him "Simon, Simon," God calls each of us by name. We can't rely on what we know about Jesus from our parents, grandparents, pastors, teachers, friends, or leaders. We must know Him personally and always keep Him as our first love.

Throughout the passages we covered, Scripture describes why this can be difficult. It's because hard times can make for hard people, and growing cold to God is sneaky. Though we start out pliable in His hands, it's easy to allow the trauma of the day, week, month, or year to affect us. If we do, we'll drift until our hearts have moved far from God and grown hard toward Him.

Thank God that in one of the hardest hours of humanity, Jesus is calling *you* by name. He's calling *you* toward salvation. He's calling *you* to embrace godly fear and repentance that will bring unexplainable peace to your heart and undeniable restoration to your life.

IT'S SPIRITUAL

After speaking to Peter seriously and specifically, Jesus proves one more point with His address. He says, "Indeed, Satan has asked for you, that he may sift *you* as wheat. But I have prayed for you, that your faith should not fail; and when you have returned to *Me,* strengthen your brethren" (Luke 22: 31, 32). It confirms what we said at the beginning of our chapter. The hour we live in is spiritual. It's a kingdom battle, a supernatural standoff. In this same passage, Jesus gives Peter the key to enduring the times: faith.

A few chapters earlier, in Luke 18, Jesus told The Parable of the Persistent Widow to encourage people to pray with persistence. In the story, a widow pursues justice with a judge until he settles her matter. Jesus closed out His teaching by asking the people, "Will not God bring about justice for his chosen ones, who cry out to him day and night? Will he keep putting them off? I tell you, he will see that they get justice and quickly. However, when the Son of Man comes, will he find faith on the earth?"

Like in this parable, faith is the key to persisting in every season. Not the lukewarm faith of Laodecia but pure, genuine faith. Paul describes how we know our faith is genuine when he wrote, "We

> "A faith tested through fire is a faith that can be trusted."

can rejoice, too, when we run into problems and trials, for we know they help us develop endurance. And endurance develops strength of character, and character strengthens our confident hope of salvation" (Romans 5:3-4 NLT).

A faith tested through fire is a faith that can be trusted. Paul also wrote:

> In this you greatly rejoice, though now for a little while, if need be, you have been grieved by various trials, that the genuineness of your faith, being much more precious than gold that perishes, though it is tested by fire, may be found to result in praise, honor, and glory at the revelation of Jesus Christ, whom having not seen you love. Though now you do not see Him, yet believing, you rejoice with joy inexpressible and full of glory, receiving the end of your faith—the salvation of your souls (1 Peter 1:6-9 ESV).

When made genuine through trial, our faith will outlast any problem that may come our way. Yes, it might be the hour of peril, but it's also the hour of deliverance! It might be a day of trouble, but it's also a day of praise. When we discern the hour and pursue authentic faith, God *will* keep us until the end. We may not have seen the battle's end, but He is already singing songs of our deliverance.

BUY, DON'T SELL

I'm not an avid investor, but even the most amateur one has heard that an unstable stock market is the best time to buy stocks and the worst time to sell them. That's because if you sell your investments at the market's low point, you'll get something of lesser value than if you had endured the instability. In short, you'll be giving up what you want most (a bigger account balance that produces lasting security later) for what you want now (a smaller account balance that produces an immediate, false sense of security).

> "We may not have seen the battle's end, but He is already singing songs of our deliverance."

As we've established, we're living in unstable times, but we're not just buying and selling money; we're buying and selling truth. When times are good, we buy it, continually investing in our spiritual account. But when times become unstable, we want to sell that truth for *our* "truth"—something of much lesser value. Sometimes we do this to make sense of our circumstances or to feel good in trouble. But we're called to much more than that. God wants us to continually buy and *keep* the truth, holding on to it through every changing season. Only then can we gain the true security that comes from living God's way.

It is not a simple thing to do, especially in a world full of opinions about what truth is: "... and they will turn their ears away from truth, and be turned aside to fables" (2 Timothy 4:4). Today, fables look like too many podcasts and YouTube videos. Too many opinions and too little time for prayer. We don't need to debate the smallest nuance of our faith; we need to apply the truth of the Scripture we know, walking free from any pride.

So how do we buy and keep the truth and do it continually? Commit to three things. First, study Scripture regularly, asking the Holy Spirit to help you understand it. Then, develop a disciplined prayer life, seeking God in everything. Third, spend Sundays in church, gathering with other believers to hear the Word of the Lord. Just like Noah built an ark to save his family from a day of terror, I believe the church is an ark to shelter us from and strengthen us in the times in which we live.

I think it's interesting that the first church began in a rough hour of humanity. Jesus could have saved first-century believers from the persecution of the Roman Empire, but He chose not to. Instead, He built the church and taught them to buy and hold truth. These believers' consistent investment in truth changed the people of their community, eventually spreading their faith worldwide.

I strongly believe Jesus wants a similar thing to happen today. I don't believe a Great Awakening is coming to America through political reform. I believe it's coming through the church waking up to truth once again, and this time, resolving to never let it go. I believe that this revival of the church will cause a move of God to sweep America, advancing from the pulpit to the pews to the public. America's not our savior; Jesus is. And He's counting on us just like He counted on the first church. We've got to get back to seeking truth above all else, holding on to it with all we have.

In a time of everyone finding their own "truth," let me once again draw you back to reality: according to John 14:6, Jesus *is* the truth. He's the *only* One who is completely faithful. No other system, church, politician, school, podcast, or person can give you what He gives you. So let's put our lives in the hands of the One who will care for them well throughout every season. Let's align ourselves with His Word because

"America's not our savior; Jesus is."

we know it will bring about our best life. Let's invest in what matters!

SERVE WITH PASSION

So now we see it: the signs are all there, and the solutions are obvious. We've got to discern that the hour is serious, specific, and spiritual. Then, we've got to seize our opportunity. We've got to buy the truth and never sell it, deciding once and for all that we will serve the Lord. As believers, though, we're not just called to serve the Lord however we want to. We're supposed to serve Him consistently and with passion. First Timothy 4:1 says, "Now the Spirit expressly says that in latter times some will depart from the faith, giving heed to deceiving spirits and doctrines of demons."

Many Bible scholars pause and ponder the meaning of two of these words: *Spirit* and *expressly*. Since Paul wrote these words, one must assume that they were prophetic. Albert Barnes, a highly-known theologian in the 1800s, articulated his thoughts on this verse, which is hard to deny.

> It is not quite certain, from this passage, whether the apostle means to say that this was a revelation then made to him, or whether it was a well-understood thing as taught by the Holy Spirit. He (Paul) refers to this same prophecy, and John also more than once mentions it; compare 2 Thessalonians 2; 1 John 2:18, Revelation 20:1-15...

Barnes concludes his thoughts with these words:

> From 2 Thessalonians 2:5, it would seem that this was a truth which had before been communicated to the apostle Paul and that he had dwelt on it when he preached the gospel in Thessalonica. However, there is no improbability in the suppo-

sition that so important a subject was communicated directly by the Holy Spirit to others of the apostles.[10]

The Greek word *rhetos* (translated "expressly" in 2 Timothy 4:1) is only mentioned once in the Bible. It was used very rarely in classical Greek, and Strongs 4490 tells us it means outspoken, distinctly, and expressly.[11] By definition, it means outspoken, unmistakenly, specifically, and unequivocally.

With this in mind, you can sense the force in the Spirit's words. Now more than ever, the Holy Spirit wants to be louder than every other voice in our lives, and He wants to help us live with similar devotion. While religion tells us to keep quiet, He wants us to speak out boldly and live passionately for Him.

A wonderful picture of the miracles this lifestyle can produce is found in the story of blind Bartimaeus in Mark 10:46-52. Desperate for healing, Bartimaeus called out to Jesus emphatically, causing a stir in the group of people around him. They insisted he quiet down, but he knew his miracle was close, so he got louder. He would not bypass his chance for a life change, and his ardor paid off. Jesus heard him and healed him.

That's the passion we need to serve God in these challenging days. In a time where it's easy to get distracted, we must zero in on the only thing that matters—the only One who can bring miracles into our lives and the lives of those we love: God. His faithfulness. His truth. Amid the mess, He wants to bring a miracle. Amid the uncertainty, He wants to bring peace, protection, and assurance.

Keep in mind as you pursue this passion that it's not equal to perfection. True service will never come from striving; it will only come from one thing. And I believe that in this hour, this one thing is the absolute wisest thing you can do.

CHAPTER THREE

THE WISEST THING YOU CAN DO

THE POETIC BOOKS Job, Psalms, Proverbs, Ecclesiastes, and the Song of Solomon don't recount historical experiences like most of the other Old Testament books do; rather, they tell of the heart's experiences. They probe intensely into essential questions about God, life, and love. These books also tell us that wisdom is a necessary tool for building a healthy, happy life. But God's wisdom? It's the most valuable thing we can ever acquire.

One of those books—Proverbs—is dedicated entirely to this topic. Throughout it, Solomon encourages us to seek God's wisdom (Proverbs 4:5), and he says that those who do love life (Proverbs 19:8 NIV).

God's wisdom goes beyond what makes sense to our natural minds. It gives us the upper hand over the enemy, catapulting us into God's purposes both now and for eternity. This inner leading is a divine grace helping us understand what we can't see. God's wisdom un-complicates what seems complicated regarding our relationships, finances, health, and career. It not only makes the right decisions clear, but it makes the process of walking out those decisions enjoyable, too. Because, as God says, His burden is easy, and His yoke is light. When we walk His way, we stay at a pace of grace, able and excited to fulfill all He has called us to do and be.

In the previous chapters, we considered what we've lost as a culture and discussed how we could see our lives, families, and communities restored. We highlighted the importance of discerning the hour we're in and understanding that it's serious, specific, and spiritual. Then we said that we should seize every opportunity to serve God passionately. We pointed out that this wouldn't happen by striving; instead, there is something else we would have to give ourselves to, which is the wisest thing we could ever do. So now that we've defined wisdom from God's point of view, I'll tell you what it is.

In the first four words of Psalm 116:1-2, the writer gives us the answer when he utters a simple yet powerful statement: "I love the Lord."

Love the Lord. That's the wisest thing we can do at

this hour. It's more vital than *any* other choice we can make. It's more important to our kids' futures than what school district we live in and more crucial to our marriage than any retreat or conference we attend. It's more essential to our career than any degree or position we acquire and more important to our purpose than any dream we pursue. We *must* allow our passion for God to stir within us to the point that we can't keep it to ourselves. We *must* become so impassioned that we stand up in a disengaged culture and vehemently claim, "I love the Lord!"

This is not just my opinion; it's scriptural. It's so important to Jesus that it was one of the last statements He gave to Israel while on earth. The religious leaders asked Him, "What is the greatest commandment?" And Jesus responded in Matthew 22:37-40 saying, "'You shall love the Lord your God with all your heart, with all your soul, and with all your mind.' This is the first and great commandment. And the second is like it: 'You shall love your neighbor as yourself.' On these two commandments hang all the Law and the Prophets."

It's easy to skim past this passage, assuming that because we serve God, we've got it covered, but let's stop and think about it for a moment. Do we *really* love the Lord with all our hearts? Is He our priority? Do we *really* love Him with all our souls? Is our affection for Him the same on good and hard days? Do we *really* love the Lord with all our minds, dwelling on His thoughts daily?

Jesus is clear that if we miss this, we miss it all. One day, this world will pass away. Our cars, homes, and all the world's treasures will be meaningless. The only thing that will matter for all eternity is the answer to the question: *Did I love the Lord?*

Only you and God know the answer; however, as with any love, actions give clues to affection. Think about it. When we love someone, they remain at the forefront of our minds. We spend as much time with them as possible and talk about them constantly. We look for ways to show them our love. We build our lives around them. The same attributes should translate to our relationship with the Lord. As Psalm 105:4 says, we should seek Him continually, pursuing Him with passion.

In Psalm 103:7 (ESV), we read that God "made known his ways to Moses, his acts to the people of Israel." Moses knew God's *ways*; the Israelites just knew His *works*. Moses knew who God *was*; the Israelites knew what He *did*. I don't know about you, but I don't just want to know God's *works*; I want to know His *ways*. I want to know *Him*. As we desire the Lord above all else, we will pursue Him. And as we pursue Him, He *will* make Himself known to us.

I know it's not always easy to desire the Lord like this. Maybe you weren't raised to know Him this way, so it's not natural for you. Maybe you want to experience this love, but you can't seem to overcome sinful habits keeping you distant. Or maybe you've been so hurt by people who claim to love Him that it makes you wary to open yourself up. If any of these describe you, know my heart breaks for what you have experienced. But also know: there is still hope.

You *can* live in the indescribable joy of an intimate relationship with the Lord. But first, you must recognize the absolute nature of this commitment. Our relationship with Him is not meant to be seasonal; it's designed for the long haul. Until we commit completely, we'll always be wanting for something more.

Psalm 116:1-2 continues with both an explanation and a commitment: "I love the Lord because he hears my voice and my prayer for mercy. Because he bends down to listen, I will pray as long as I have breath!" (NLT). The first thing to note is the passion with which the author penned these words. Notice the exclamation point at the end, signifying intense emotion. The second is that we don't know the author of this psalm. I love this because we can read the verse with a sense of ownership. I can say enthusiastically *that I, Matthew Pollock, love the Lord!*

> "Actions give clues to affection."

Just like in an earthly relationship, when we passionately love the Lord, there are things we will do differently. There are also things we don't do. Because we love the Lord, we will be faithful to Him. We will resist temptation. Even when our hearts are shattered, we won't give up. Even when our faith is tested, we will continue in belief.

You read the discouraging statistics in the first chapter, and I told you I believed they wouldn't be final. But ultimately, whether that's true depends upon us. God won't force us to love Him, nor will He force us to love ourselves or others. But when we truly experience God's love—recognizing it as the most massive gift we have ever been and ever will be given—we will *want* to give it back. As Paul wrote in 2 Corinthians 5:14, God's love will compel us to offer ours in return.

> "Our relationship with Jesus is not meant to be seasonal; it's designed for the long haul."

This is what will change the statistics. It's what will change our world. People say we need a revival of *faith in* God, but I believe we need a revival of *love for* God. When we get that right, the faith will come.

You might think, I *want* to have that passion for the Lord. I am ready to love Him with everything I am, but how? The writer of Psalm 116 answers this when he says, "I love the Lord *because he hears my voice and my prayer for mercy.*" The psalmist reminds himself of the Lord's goodness and faithfulness. When we, too, intentionally and continually focus on God's goodness, it draws us into a deeper appreciation for Him.

In another psalm, the psalmist David expresses the tenderest expression of his love toward God: "I love you, O Lord, my strength. The Lord is my rock and my fortress and my deliverer, my God, my rock, in whom I take refuge, my shield, and the horn of my salvation, my stronghold. I call upon the Lord, who is worthy to be praised, and I am saved from my enemies (Psalm 18:1-3 ESV)." In loving the Lord above all else, we trade our weakness for His strength, our shortcomings for His grace.

It's important to mention that in this process of falling deeper in love with the Lord, we won't be perfect. But thank God, His love covers our weaknesses. King David is an example of this. Scripture calls him a man after God's own heart. He messed up many times and in big ways, but he genuinely loved the Lord more than anything or anyone else. His relationship wasn't just for show or royal popularity points. Even when he sinned, he repented and returned to God, never allowing anything to ultimately stand between him and his first love.

Before we continue, I encourage you to reflect for a few moments. Take an honest assessment of your heart. Who or what has it? Does God have it? Does

> "People say we need a revival of faith in God, but I believe we need a revival of love for God. When we get that right, the faith will come."

another person have it? What about money? Fame and power? Pride or insecurity? Fear and worry? Do you desire the things of God that will produce for all eternity?

Or do you seek carnal things that will end with your life? Can you honestly and confidently put your name in the passage, passionately declaring that *you* love the Lord?

A LOVELESS PLAGUE

If your answer is no, I don't want you to be discouraged; I do, however, want you to be sober. You may be in this place by accident or unawareness but understand: it *is* a choice. *Your* choice. You have two roads before you, and the one you take will make an eternal difference. The first road is the path to intentionally falling more in love with the Lord. Just as you would choose to fall more in love with a person by pursuing them, spending time with them, and meditating on what you love about them, you can do the same with God. The second path is to continue in a lack of love.

If the latter is the road you choose, I want you to be aware of what you're choosing. Paul makes it clear when he writes, "If anyone has no love for the Lord, let him be accursed" (1 Corinthians 16:22 ESV).

The word *accursed* comes from the Greek word *anathema*, which means "devoted to destruction."[12] When we choose not to wholly love our Creator, we give the enemy permission to do as he pleases in our life. We submit ourselves to his satanic plan, and his plan always equals destruction. This loveless plague wreaks havoc on our homes, causing fear to replace faith, hate to replace love, striving to replace grace, and worry to replace trust. The list goes on, but the bottom line is this: When the enemy runs things, we end up unloved, unhappy, and unhealthy. When God takes over, everything changes.

Here's the beautiful thing: *you* and *only* you have the power to open and close the door to the enemy. So, I urge you, with everything in me, to choose the wisest way. Shut the door once and for all, resolving every day to love the Lord with all you are. It's your greatest privilege and most secure protection. But it's also your choice. *You* are the one that must pursue and protect this love.

I realize you might still not know where your love for Christ stands. You may say, "I think I'm on the right road, but I don't quite have the passion of the psalmist. The love might be there, but I'm not sure it's where it needs to be." If so, let's gain clarity together. Scripture helps us gauge our position by describing three major types of lacking love. Let's identify them and then discuss how to return to the path of persistent pursuit.

> "When the enemy runs things, we end up unloved, unhappy, and unhealthy. When God takes over, everything changes."

ABSENT LOVE

The first major lacking love is obvious. It's absent love,

the kind chosen by an unbeliever. As a whole, America falls under this category. Most of the cultural issues we want to chalk up to "sin" problems are really more like "absent love" problems. As we previously discussed, our nation has grown cold to the things of God, and our callousness has brought destruction upon us. It's an epidemic, but I am believing we will see a turnaround. Many of you are believing for the same—that as we embrace a love for God again, we *will* see Him move in ways that believers for generations have prayed for.

If you fall under the "absent love" category, please know God is not mad at you. He actually feels just the opposite. You're in His heart and mind constantly. He longs for His great love to compel you to love Him in return. If you desire this, I invite you to turn to the back of the book and pray the prayer of salvation with me. The decision to make Jesus your Lord and Savior is the most important one you will ever make.

We see a wonderful example of the Lord's unrelenting love in Peter's story. After pledging his loyalty to Jesus just days earlier, Peter's love was tested. The story is found in John 18. Judas had just betrayed Jesus, handing Him over to the religious leaders in the Garden of Gethsemane. Jesus was brought for questioning before Caiaphas, the high priest. Peter stood outside the courtyard door, awaiting the trial's outcome. While there, several people associated Peter with Jesus, asking, "You also are not one of his disciples, are you?"

Peter thought his association with Jesus might threaten his physical safety, so he denied knowing Him three times. I can only imagine the remorse he felt in the days after as Jesus was persecuted and eventually crucified. To know he could turn away from someone who loved him so greatly, purely, and devotedly had to produce feelings of deep regret. But as He always does, Jesus gave Peter a second chance. After His resurrection, in John 21:15-17 (ESV), Jesus asked Peter three times, "Simon, son of John, do you love me?"

Two things stand out about Jesus' response that represents His restorative nature. First, He called Peter by name. This let Peter know that Jesus still saw and loved him, despite the path he had previously chosen. Second, Jesus gave Peter the opportunity for total restoration, asking the question three times—the same number of times he had denied Him.

If you find yourself with an absent love for the Lord, I want you to hear this passage of Scripture with your name in place of Peter's. Jesus is calling *you* by name to come into a relationship with Him. He promises He will wipe away your past, restoring every regret you've ever had. All you have to do is respond.

DRIFTING LOVE

The second type of love that falls short is drifting love. We fall into this category when we once loved God passionately, but the passion has waned. Most of the time, those in this category know much about God but may not truly know Him. At one time, they might have, but they stopped the pursuit, perhaps getting stuck in a cycle of religion.

If this is you, I want to be frank: you're on the same dangerous ground the people in Matthew 7 walked. You're not *absent*, but you're also not *passionate*. You're lukewarm. This is hazardous because you're probably comfortable, and you'll likely never change unless you see the peril in your situation. *This* is your warning sign. Do not allow your education of God to pull you away from fully experiencing Him. Dive once again into divine pursuit.

Second Chronicles 25 gives a list of kings and describes how they ruled. If you skim the chapter, you'll find that one led right, then one led wrong, then a couple led right, then a couple led wrong. The cycle continues throughout the whole passage. It's sobering to see how these leaders, who had all been taught God's ways, grew comfortable enough to compromise.

One king, Amaziah, was 25 years old when he assumed the kingship. He reigned in Jerusalem for 29 years, and though he initially loved God, his love drifted. "He did right in the sight of the LORD, yet not with a whole heart" (2 Chronicles 25:2 NASB 1995). Amaziah did many things scripturally right, but the nation failed under him because he didn't love God wholly.

You too can do many things right, checking all the

religious boxes off your list, but if you're not careful, over time, while your hand is working for God, your heart will drift far from Him. A once beautiful, passionate love will become a mundane obligation, opening the door for the enemy to wreak havoc in your life and in your family. The worst part is you may not even realize it. I urge you today to wake up from this place of apathy and run once again to the greatest love you'll ever be offered.

REPLACED LOVE

The third type of love that falls short is common among believers and has been since the beginning. I imagine nearly every one of us has found ourselves here at one time or another. This kind of love replaces our *first* love with a *lesser* love. That lesser love could be money, power, or fame. Or it could be something important to God—like family, serving in our local church, or even pursuing His call on our life.

While these things are good, we must understand that they are not the main thing, and it is imperative that we keep our priorities straight. As Matthew 6:33 says, as we seek the Lord first, all other things will be added unto us. When we make loving God the priority, everything else lines up as it's meant to be.

In 2 Timothy 3, Paul prophetically listed things that would threaten our love for Christ in these last days. He said we would be tempted to love ourselves first, putting our desires ahead of God's. He said we would be tempted to love pleasure first, seeking only to make ourselves happy. Paul also said we would be tempted to love money first, compromising for an opportunity. To that point, please understand that the enemy will pay you any amount to keep you out of God's will. He knows how valuable you are to God and His kingdom. In his eyes, no amount is too great if it will keep you distracted from the prime purpose of loving your Maker.

> **"The enemy will pay you any amount to keep you out of God's will. He knows how valuable you are."**

If you recognize yourself in any of these categories, take heart: today can be the day things change. This moment can be your defining moment— your *Abraham moment.*

AN ABRAHAM MOMENT

It's encouraging to know that even one of the most well-known fathers of our faith, Abraham, had to keep a close watch on his priorities. Though Scripture doesn't state it explicitly, it leads us to believe that Abraham's heart may have begun veering from his love for God toward a lesser love. This lesser love was a good thing. It was his son, Isaac.

Abraham had believed for Isaac for 25 years. His wife Sarah miraculously gave birth to him in her old age. Isaac was the beautiful fulfillment of God's promise to him, and Abraham loved him deeply. When Isaac was on the verge of his teenage years, God asked Abraham for something that made no sense to him. He asked for Isaac back, instructing Abraham to sacrifice his most precious gift on the altar. It sounds terrible, but before Jesus came to earth as the Ultimate Sacrifice, people had to sacrifice animals to atone for their sins. God wasn't asking for Isaac's life to be cruel; He was testing Abraham's priorities.

In perhaps one of the most destiny-defining moments of his life, Abraham chose to remain faithful. He arose early in the morning and traveled with Isaac to the top of the mountain. After gathering the wood, Abraham cut it, placed it on the altar, and put Isaac on top of it. Just as Abraham lifted the knife to sacrifice his son, an angel called out to stop him.

> "But the angel of the Lord called to him from heaven and said, 'Abraham, Abraham!' And he said, 'Here I am.' He said, 'Do not lay your hand on the boy or do anything to him, for now I know that you fear God, seeing you have not withheld your son, your only son, from me'" (Genesis 22:11-12 ESV).

Because Abraham chose well at this moment, prioritizing God above all else, he closed the door on the enemy, prohibiting him from working in his life. Instead, God worked mightily in Abraham's life, in Isaac's life, and in the lives of those in the generations that followed.

You, too, will have an Abraham moment. You may have several throughout your lifetime. They definitely won't require human sacrifice, but God will undoubtedly, in some way, ask you: "Who is first in your life? Will you put me above that opportunity? Will you put me above that relationship?" And when, like Abraham, you choose God first, He will bless you immeasurably.

Throughout Scripture, we read about many fathers of our faith making destiny-defining decisions. The most important of all was Jesus. In Matthew 26:39 (ESV), we meet Him at the point of decision. Referring to His imminent crucifixion, Jesus prayed, "... My Father, if it be possible, let this cup pass from me; nevertheless, not as I will, but as you will."

Jesus didn't *want* to die, but He chose to love God more than He loved Himself. He chose to put Him first. This decision set Jesus on His path of destiny to become the Savior of the world. Though He endured great momentary pain through the crucifixion, He was resurrected and is now seated with the Father in heaven, ruling and reigning for eternity.

About eight years ago, I encountered one of my life's biggest Abraham moments when a pastor I deeply admire approached me three times about leaving our church to become a campus pastor for him. By then, I had invested several years in our church, and the congregation had also invested much in our family. God had moved greatly at The Way, and I didn't feel He was done. So though the opportunity was amazing, and I felt honored, the first two times this pastor asked, I said no. The third time he approached me, I felt the Lord tell me to go but not to close the doors of The Way.

So, that's what we did. After laying out a six-month plan, my family and I stepped out in faith, moving halfway across the country. God was faithful throughout those six months, and the new church seemed to explode overnight. We've never seen anything like it in our ministry before. I was preaching to thousands weekly and traveling with the pastor, who had become one of my greatest heroes. But then, the unexpected happened. Strategy began to change, and I didn't feel I fit anymore. The peace was gone. After praying it through, I knew what God was saying: it was time to return to The Way.

It was one of the toughest decisions of my life. To this day, I love this pastor and friend. I didn't want to hurt him, but I knew I had to follow God. So, I approached my hero and bore my heart to him, telling him what God had shown me. I had to leave behind what seemed to be the opportunity of a lifetime. I didn't necessarily *want* to give it up, but I knew what God was asking of me. I knew this was an Abraham Moment.

This pastor was gracious with me and blessed my return home. When we arrived, I was devastated by what I found. The Way was barely functioning. About 75% of the people had left. Those who remained were back to meeting in a school rather than the beautiful building we had met in. I wasn't sure I would have an income from pastoring; I thought I might have to find a second job.

The next six months were *hard*. I felt defeated. Almost daily, I woke up with thoughts of *What have I done?* It took nearly everything in me to stand in the pulpit and preach on Sundays. Abby had to carry me through that season, reminding me consistently that I had chosen God's way and He would be faithful, as He has always been. We must all be careful not to judge these Abraham moments too quickly. Though we probably won't see the fruit immediately, as Paul encourages us in Galatians 6:9, "... in due season, we will reap, if we do not give up."

That's exactly what happened to us. Six months after returning to The Way, we obtained a new building, and everything began to turn around. God has proven himself faithful day after day as we have continually committed ourselves to Him. That doesn't mean it was easy, though. Abraham Moments never are. But when we choose to love God above all else, He *will* come through for us, just as He did for Abraham, just as He did for me, and just as He will for you.

I don't know where your love for God stands today. Maybe it's absent, maybe it has drifted, or maybe it's being replaced by a lesser love. Wherever you are, again, please understand: *this* can be your Abraham moment.

Today, *you* can decide to love God above all else and never stop pursuing Him.

I realize you might have already made this decision. You may be entirely in love with the Lord. If so, I celebrate with you! I also encourage you to keep pursuing Him with passion. One of the most beautiful characteristics of this divine relationship is that with God, you can always go deeper. You can always climb higher.

TAKE IT DEEPER

If you've ever hiked a mountain, you know it takes work, but the views are more than worth it. In the same way, it's work to climb higher with God, building greater intimacy with Him. It takes effort to pursue His presence, but the result makes the labor feel trivial. Psalm 24:3-5 speaks of this journey: "Who may ascend into the hill of the Lord? Or who may stand in His holy place? He who has clean hands and a pure heart, Who has not lifted up his soul to an idol, Nor sworn deceitfully. He shall receive blessing from the Lord, And righteousness from the God of his salvation."

If your love for the Lord already fits Matthew 22's description, I encourage you to climb higher. Yes, this will require a new level of commitment. You'll have to say *no* to more things you want to say *yes* to and *yes* to more things you want to say *no* to, many of which may not even be wrong. But I promise you: what is at the top of that hill is worth it.

In verse four, the psalmist gives the qualifications for who is eligible to climb the hill of a deeper relationship with Christ. It says, "He who has clean hands and a pure heart, Who has not lifted up his soul to an idol, Nor sworn deceitfully." These sample qualities do not signify a sinless or perfect life but a heart like David's, Abraham's, and Jesus'—one in constant pursuit of God, with an incessant desire to please Him.

As with choosing to love God initially, climbing higher is a choice; it requires intentionality. Remember: Jesus was the closest to God anyone on earth ever has been, and even *He* had to make a choice.

In John 6, we read about feasts being held throughout Israel for Passover. After performing a series of miracles, instead of enjoying the feasts, Jesus left the people and climbed a mountainside to pray. He could have stayed with the people. It wouldn't have been wrong. But He wanted to go deeper with God, so He chose to climb the mountain.

Now, let me be clear: God wants us to enjoy life. But He also wants us to be so set on going higher with Him that we desire *Him* more than material things—even *good* material things. If we do, the outcome will make us much happier than material things ever could have.

If you continue through chapter six, you'll find it was on this mountain that Jesus performed one of His greatest miracles—feeding 5,000 men with only five loaves of bread and two fish. But guess what? Only those who followed Jesus up the mountain experienced it. Friends, for undeniable, miraculous encounters with God, you must climb mountains. You will have to make the destiny-defining decision to leave behind what's easy.

Wherever you find yourself today, the call is both apparent and urgent. You know the wisest thing to do in this hour. So, what will you choose? My greatest hope is that in a time of undeniable apathy, you'll choose to stand and passionately claim, "I love the Lord!" Then, I pray you'll resolve in every season to keep climbing higher.

If you've made this decision, I want to end by saying two things. First, congratulations! You have officially started, restarted, or committed to continuing the most beautiful journey of your life. Second, welcome. I know this road gets a little narrower the higher you climb, but it gets more beautiful, too. You'll see. So, come on, let's go. Let's journey together along the Way of Truth!

> "For undeniable, miraculous encounters with God, you must climb mountains. You will have to make the destiny-defining decision to leave behind what's easy."

CHAPTER FOUR

WELCOME TO THE WAY

IN THE LAST chapter, we studied Psalm 116, where the psalmist makes a passionate, prophetic statement of love for the Lord. King David did the same in Psalm 119:30-32 when he wrote: "I have chosen the way of truth; Your judgments I have laid before me. I cling to Your testimonies; O Lord, do not put me to shame! I will run the course of Your commandments, For You shall enlarge my heart." Another passage talks about the same path when it says, "And many will follow their sensuality, and because of them, the way of truth will be blasphemed" (2 Peter 2:2 ESV). The Way of Truth mentioned in both passages is the same one you just committed (or recommitted) to following.

Life is made up of choices like these—choices about how we are going to live. Every day, we choose whether or not we will serve the Lord and to what degree we will do it. We choose whether or not we are going to trust God and to what extent. David made his choice clear by beginning his declaration with, "I have chosen!" If you study the time he lived in, you'll find the reason for this. It's because David made his choice in contrast to many around him. His generation was much like ours, filled with wickedness and deceit. But as we have, he passionately declared he would choose a different way, *the* Way.

As we've established, this path is called *the* Way because there is *only* one way. While many ascribe to the popular belief that you have "your truth" and I have "my truth," we must constantly remind ourselves that there is only *one* truth—the truth revealed in the work God accomplished through Jesus Christ.

The Way is the greatest, safest path you could ever take. Here, everyone fits, and everyone belongs. All ages, stages, races, genders, and backgrounds are invited. We find everything we need here. Even the deepest God-planted wishes of our hearts are waiting for us as we advance into the beautiful life He has planned. Oh, what a place to be!

If you've made it to this chapter, then at some point in your life, you heard the beautiful sound of the Way calling you, beckoning you to a new life in Christ. You responded, choosing the Way of Truth. But now, I must ask—how far have you made it down the path? Are your shoes well-worn from walking? Have you yet to begin? Have you tried making progress but feel stuck? No matter how far you've traveled, know two things. First, there is absolutely no condemnation on the Way. Second, you can start making progress *today*.

To do so, you've got to commit wholeheartedly to God's process for progress. So as we travel down this glorious path together, I invite you to pray King David's prayer of commitment with me. Then, I encourage you to continue praying this prayer daily. "Teach me your way, O Lord, that I may walk in your truth; unite my heart to fear your name" (Psalm 86:11 ESV).

Now that we understand more about the Way, let me introduce you to two vital tools you'll need along its path.

OUR GUIDE

The first is a relationship with the Guide. You can't see Him, but you can hear and feel Him. His name is the Spirit of Truth, also known as the Holy Spirit. His job is to ensure we make all the right turns, staying safely on the Way. The more we invest in this relationship, the more progress we'll make.

Our Guide is necessary because, on the Way, we can't live by our thoughts. If we try, we won't last. The internal conflict between our will and God's will becomes too much to bear, and we will take a detour at some point. However, if we commit to listening to our Guide, God's will eventually *becomes* our will. Here's how it works: the more we listen to our Guide, the more we think like Him and begin desiring what we're meant to have. And the more we desire the things we're meant to have, the more God will give us our heart's desires.

OUR MAP

The second tool is our Map, the Word of Truth, also known as the Bible. You may be familiar with it already. It's humanity's most reliable ancient document, which is what David wrote much of Psalm 119 about. In this chapter, he pens a transparent articulation of his desire for the Word, which he calls a "great treasure." He also uses four other words to describe it: judgments, precepts, commandments, and ordinances.

Unlike David, some who have walked the Way have doubted whether God was the author of this Map. Unfortunately, those people haven't made it to the end. While God inspired men to write the words down, they are *His* infallible words. "All Scripture is breathed out by God and profitable for teaching, for reproof, for correction, and for training in righteousness, that the man of God may be complete, equipped for every good work" (2 Timothy 3:16-17).

Before we progress any farther down the Way, each of us must decide what we think of our Map. Do we believe what 1 Peter 1:23 says—that it is the living, imperishable truth authored by God? Do we believe its words are final? We might as well turn around now if the answer to either is no. Because without the clarity of this map, we're doomed to take a detour. It's these words that will keep us on the Way. "They are not just idle words for you—they are your life" (Deuteronomy 32:47 NIV).

Now that we have met our Guide and have our Map, it's time to start walking.

START WALKING

In previous chapters, we discovered the importance of discerning and deciding. We've had to discern the hour we live in and decide the path we will walk. Now, it's time to apply. We've got to put our decision into action and start traveling on the Way of Truth.

As we walk, I need to make two things clear. The first is that along the Way, you will find many opportunities to learn and progress. That's because, as a culture, we've never had more knowledge at our fingertips. From YouTube messages to e-books to virtual Bible studies, opportunities for growth abound. Know this, though: if that knowledge is not applied, you won't get very far. It will always be what you *apply*, not simply what you *know*, that will transform your life. Known *and* applied truth equals freedom and progress. This application has to be personal, too. As much as I wish my application of knowledge could set you free, it can't; no one's can. You *must* apply it for yourself.

The second thing to clarify is that, just as there are many opportunities to grow along the Way, there's also an adversary trying to blind you to those opportunities. "And even if our gospel is veiled, it is veiled to those who are perishing. In their case the god of this world has blinded the minds of the unbelievers, to keep them from seeing the light of the gospel of the glory of Christ, who is the image of God" (2 Corinthians 4:3-4 ESV). Satan knows that in whatever area you are blind to the truth, you'll stay stuck. So his greatest attack is to keep you unaware of what you need.

> "Known *and* applied truth equals freedom and progress."

He has done this to me in one of my life's most precious areas—my marriage. When I was younger, the enemy tried desperately to blind me to the love of my wife. He knew her love was my most valuable gift outside of Jesus—one that would help me walk in all He had for me. So, the enemy attempted to shield me from seeing it. Abby has always shown love well; it was certainly nothing she did. However, I still struggled, constantly questioning whether her love was genuine. It didn't take long to see that my insecurity stagnated our growth as a couple, diminishing the freedom and fruitfulness of our marriage.

Thankfully, the truth broke through. One day, while praying, I received a revelation from God through Scripture and finally saw the truth about my situation.

I didn't just accept the knowledge, though; I acted on it, too. I stopped letting the lies talk; instead, I declared what God had shown me. It wasn't the revelation that changed things; it was the application of it. It was when I applied the truth I had learned that I made progress. That's what applied truth does. It dissolves the very fabric of falsehoods and brings true freedom.

Now that we're walking, there is one more thing I want to draw your attention to: the signs.

THE YIELD SIGN

There are only two types of signs you'll find on the Way. The first is the yield sign. David abstractly refers to this sign in his words, "I will run the course of Your commandments, For You shall enlarge my heart" (Psalm 119:32).

When followed, the yield sign produces progress, but understand that progress looks different on this path. Here, internal progress comes *before* external progress. As David calls it, the "enlarging" of our hearts comes before physical advancement. As we implement God's instruction, applying His knowledge to our situation, He enlarges our hearts.

> "Applied truth dissolves the very fabric of falsehoods and brings true freedom."

The Hebrew word *rachab* (translated as "enlarge" in Psalm 119:32) means to grow wide, to expand, to open wide as a result of removing hindering factors, to make adjustments to, and to set free.[13] It is what happens when we apply truth, allowing God to transform our hearts. The enlargement opens wide our once closed-off hearts, bringing healing, wholeness, and freedom from every bondage. It increases our capacity to handle anything we might encounter along the way, enabling us to move forward.

I love what Proverbs 4:18 ESV says about our journey: "... the path of the righteous is like the light of dawn, which shines brighter and brighter until full day." It's true that the farther you walk on the Way, the more narrow the path grows. But it's also true that the farther you walk on the Way, the better the path gets. So when you see a yield sign, I urge you to follow its instruction. It's the Father asking you to make a change necessary to enlarge your heart so that you can progress into the incredible future He has planned.

If you choose not to yield, you have two other options. Of course, you can stop in the middle of the road, which is dangerous. Or you can heed the other sign— the one called exit.

THE EXIT SIGN

The exit sign is the second sign you'll see along the way. Anytime you want to leave the path, the offramp is there. That's because God is not a dictator. He will never take away your ability to choose.

You'll notice that the higher we climb and the narrower the road gets, the more people choose to exit. What many don't understand is that avoiding God's yield signs doesn't keep them from having to yield. They'll either yield on the Way or on the road they're exiting onto—the Road of the Accursed. This is the road we spoke of in the last chapter. When we merge onto it, we take the path of Satan's plan for our lives, and his plans always end in destruction.

Trust me, I know it's difficult to ignore the exits. The best way to do so is to settle your heart at the beginning. Settle today that your decision to walk the Way is a *covenant*, not a *contract*. And just like in a marriage covenant, when you committed to the Way, you promised you wouldn't look elsewhere. Until death do you part, you promised to yield only to the truth.

At the beginning of your journey, you'll notice a lot of exits. But the longer you walk, and the more you adhere to the Guide, Map, and yield signs, the less attention you'll pay to them. That's because your pledge of solidarity has deemed exiting unworthy as an option. Sometimes your choice will get tested, though, especially when people you love decide to exit. That's why it's imperative to decide today what your choice will be, then act daily upon that decision. When things get tough, remember what Jesus says: "You did not choose me, but I chose you" (John 15:16 ESV). God handpicked you to walk this road. You have been custom created to handle all you will encounter. No matter who goes in the opposite direction, you must choose to stay on the path.

At first, you may not like the obvious lines on the Way. They may make you feel too different from those who walk on other roads. They might make you stand out more than you'd like. But the lines aren't bright and crisp for no reason. They are obvious by design. First

"Faith works best when it's firm."

Peter 2:9 tells us that we are to live distinctly in the land as a chosen people. Every area of our lives should look different from those not on the Way to testify of the goodness and faithfulness of God. Trust me, one day, you'll be grateful for the distinction. Because if you're faithful until the end, the distinction won't end on earth; it will live for eternity.

> Then those who feared the Lord spoke with one another. The Lord paid attention and heard them, and a book of remembrance was written before him of those who feared the Lord and esteemed his name. "They shall be mine," says the Lord of hosts, "in the day when I make up my treasured possession, and I will spare them as a man spares his son who serves him. Then once more you shall see the distinction between the righteous and the wicked, between one who serves God and one who does not serve him" (Malachi 3:16-18 ESV).

Throughout Scripture, the distinction between those who walk the Way is abundantly clear. It's also clear that the choice to live distinctly is ours. It's our decision *and* our application that will determine our eternity.

I have walked the Way for a while, and I know there will be days when an exit sign will seem like your best option. But with compassion and humility, I urge you with these words: Stay on the path, for faith works best when it's firm. Decide today and every day that there will be no sway.

CHAPTER FIVE
NO SWAY

ABBY AND I have four children, ages 16 to 25. Parenting them has offered us an up-close view of the plethora of temptations with which Gen Z gets bombarded. At every turn, the media is placing huge, flashing billboards trying to convince them there is a road better than the one they're walking. Of course, I dealt with temptation at their age and still do, as every generation and person does. But as we have discussed, we are in a unique era in which temptation seems to have intensified.

Because of this, a few years ago, I preached a message at our church called "No Sway," talking about this very thing. The thought came from 1 John 5:19, which says, "We know that we are of God, and the whole world lies *under the sway of* the wicked one." In this message, I encouraged everyone not to allow any sway in our walks with Christ along the Way. That statement stuck with my church family and my family, and throughout the years, it made its way into our everyday language.

At home, if one of our kids was going out with friends, we'd say, "Okay. Have fun! No sway." If they were starting their first day of school, we'd say, "Have a great day! And remember, no sway." It wasn't just Abby and me uttering this phrase, though; the kids gave "no sway" a life of its own, using it daily. I'd hear them often reminding each other as they hung up the phone or pulled out of the driveway—"Hey, Kaleb, no sway." Or "Hey, Hope, no sway." I'd hear them talking compassionately about a friend they were praying for, saying, "Yeah, he's in the sway, but he'll come back."

Our church family uses the phrase just as often. (There might even be a few tattoos!) Throughout these past few years, this lighthearted adage has served a serious purpose for all of us, reminding us to remain watchful of distractions and keep ourselves from the enemy's sway. We know we can't avoid seeing the signs and can't keep anyone else from seeing them, either. But we *can* remind each other that though the signs are present, we don't have to heed them.

John declares that "the *whole world* lies under the sway of the wicked one," and as a culture, we can confirm this is not an exaggeration. Just think about it: hardly anything is innocent anymore. From school systems to political agendas to marketing strategies to media in every form—*every* structure and system has been tainted by the sway, and this sway is *designed* to pull us away. The most dangerous part about swaying is that it seems innocent at first. We usually begin with just a little veer, not enough for anyone to notice. If we keep our gaze there long enough, though, the sway will lead to distraction, and the distraction will lead to a detour.

DISTRACTIONS AND DETOURS

This happened to the church of Galatia. Everything was moving wonderfully well for them until an intruder who had fallen led them astray. With this knowledge, the Apostle Paul wrote them a letter.

> You ran well. Who hindered you from obeying the truth? This persuasion does not *come* from Him who calls you. A little leaven leavens the whole lump. I have confidence in you, in the Lord, that you will have no other mind; but he who troubles you shall bear his judgment, whoever he is. And I, brethren, if I still preach circumcision, why do I still suffer persecution? Then the offense of the cross has ceased (Galatians 5:7-11).

The first thing Paul asks the Galatians is what we all ask ourselves when we realize how far we've drifted from our path. We ask, "What happened? We were doing so well! How did we end up here?" Then Paul reminds them that a little leaven leavens the whole lump. A little sway leads to a detour. Perhaps this happened in the church of Laodicea. Perhaps they began with small compromises until those small compromises drew them into a stupor of lukewarm indifference.

Here's the reality—the enemy is not dumb. His signs will not blatantly urge you to exit from the Way. Instead, he will distract you with something that seems innocent—a movie you shouldn't watch, a conversation you shouldn't engage in, or a compromise at work that no one would notice. The enemy works like this because, on his own, he's powerless. He can't *make* you take a detour. Only *you* can do that. All he can do is find an area of weakness that seems like only a simple compromise and, as Paul says, *hinder* you through distraction.

Paul often used unique Greek words to help the reader understand the meaning of his writing. He did this with the Greek word later translated *hinder*. The Greek word originally used is *egkoptó*. It means to "cut *int*o (like blocking off a road); *hinder* by 'introducing an obstacle that stands *sharply in the way of a moving object*'... *sharply impede*, by *cutting off* what is desired or needed; to block."[14]

Satan knows that when he captures your mind, even just for a minute, he hinders your journey as you sway unintentionally into distraction. The next time, he'll say, "See? No one caught you. It's not even that bad. And see how happy it made you? Now, let's try this." Then he'll persuade you to sway a bit further. This process will continue until you end up taking a detour onto his road, devoting your days to his destructive ways. Then one day, you awake to a mess, wondering how you got so off track.

As you look back on your journey, you'll realize that your detour likely didn't result from one big move. It occurred because of one little sway after another little sway. It is why we say that the sway is designed to pull you away! It's also why we must remain vigilant against the illusions of the enemy working overtime to serve as massive distractions in our lives. These illusions draw us into spiritual deception and sin, and all the while, we think we're fine. Slowly but surely, it causes us to settle into lukewarm living, just

"The sway is designed to pull you away!"

like the church of Laodicea. If we don't wake up to it on this side of eternity, we will find ourselves being rebuked, just as they were.

I don't say this to scare you. I desire for you what I desire for my family and church family. I want you to live aware of the enemy's strategies so that you steer clear of his exit signs. No one is immune to his ploys. Even the Apostle Paul was hindered! First Thessalonians 2:18 tells the story of how the enemy hindered him. But although he hindered Paul, he couldn't stop him, and he can't stop you, either. *You* decide whether you submit to the detour or avoid the sway and stay on the path God has marked out for you.

So how do we make the right choice, practically? How do we fight distractions and avoid the sway? First, we must discern those distractions, and thankfully, this is not as hard as we often think. There are a few factors to consider when deciding whether something is from God or our enemy. First, we must understand that everything in God makes progress on the Way. If the decision will cause you to regress instead, it's not God. Second, everything in God is stable. If the voice makes you feel confused or conflicted, it's not God. Lastly, everything in God is pure. If you're sensing a pull toward sin, even if it's wrapped in something that *seems* good, that is not our Guide. It is an invitation to sway.

As John 15 ends, Jesus warns the disciples that as the world hates Him, they will also hate His disciples. In the very next verse, He says, "I have said all these things to you to keep you from falling away," (John 16:1 ESV). Jesus' whole purpose in coming to earth—everything He said and did—was to ensure we would not sway but stay planted firmly on the Way of Truth. There *is* hope for us, and His name is *Jesus*!

Discerning the enemy's tactics leads us to the second thing we must do—call him out on his schemes. We must see the situation plainly and rebuke the enemy for even trying to pull us away. We should say confidently, "Oh, that offense? That's a distraction." Or "Oh, that toxic relationship trying to re-enter my life? That's an invitation to sway." Then we must fight temptation with joy. As Nehemiah wrote, "...the joy of the Lord is your strength" (Nehemiah 8:10), and we need strength daily for our walk. The key to tapping into it is through remembrance and expectancy. Remember how far God has brought you, and look forward to where He is taking you.

With each step we take, we are either walking further down the Way or further from it. We're either walking toward God or away from Him. No matter how far down the road we have traveled, every one of us is susceptible to a detour. Jonah—one of the Lord's prophets—demonstrated this with his diversion.

> "Now the word of the Lord came to Jonah the son of Amittai, saying, "Arise, go to Nineveh, that great city, and call out against it, for their evil has come up before me." But Jonah rose to flee to Tarshish from the presence of the Lord. He went down to Joppa and found a ship going to Tarshish. So he paid the fare and went down into it, to go with them to Tarshish, away from the presence of the Lord (Jonah 1:1-3).

Jonah was a prophet trusted in and used by God, and even he gave in to a detour. As it always does, Jonah's detour started with distractions—offense and pride. God instructed Jonah to travel to Nineveh and command the people to repent. He did several times, but they refused. The Lord was patient with the Ninevites, and Jonah grew tired of preaching to them with no judgment for apathy toward change. So one day, when the Lord asked him again to prophesy to Nineveh, he went the other way. That sway led him into a distraction, leading him to take a detour.

We see another example in our previously discussed story of Peter. Just before Peter denies knowing Jesus, Scripture abundantly clarifies an important truth. "Then seizing him, they led him away and took him into the house of the high priest. Peter followed at a distance" (Luke 22:54 NIV). It's an illusion to think we can follow Jesus at a distance and stand strong when the enemy comes for us! We can't! We will deny Him, too. Space leads to sway, so I urge you—remove the gap! You don't have to give way to the sway.

Instead, as Solomon reminds us in Proverbs 4:23, "Keep your heart with all diligence, For out of it *spring* the issues of life." Our hearts are the epicenter of everything the Lord desires to do in and through us. As we guard them and allow the Lord to free them from bondages and enlarge them

> "Space leads to sway, so remove the gap!"

with His truth, we leave no room for the enemy's distractions. Remember—your journey is more about what's happening *in* you than *around* you, and God will use everything *around* you to do a greater work *in* you.

There is one more truth I want to point out about our enemy, and it's this: he is a skilled pretender. He's good at making himself sound like our Guide, so if you haven't gotten to know the Guide and the Map well, you might mistake his voice for God's. Those are the times you have to remember the keys to discerning. If it's God, there will always be progress, stability, and purity, but if the opposite realities are present, it's the enemy trying to persuade you to exchange his way for the Way.

THE GOOD KIND OF FEAR

Now, I want to let you in on a truth I've discovered from years of walking the Way. I've already given you the wisest thing you can do: love the Lord. But do you know what initiates that love? Do you know what lights the flame of our ever-growing passion for God? Fearing Him. Solomon understood this when he wrote, "The fear of the LORD *is* the beginning of wisdom" (Proverbs 9:10).

This does not mean we live *afraid* of Him, though we operate with a wholesome dread of displeasing Him. What it means is that we are so in *awe* of God and His goodness that we are driven by an internal desire to walk His way. I believe the fear of the Lord is the biggest thing missing in the American church today. It's what ultimately causes a Laodicean-like lukewarmness. We should *never* lose our wonder for God, His church, and all He has given us. We should *always* tremble at the power and beauty of His Word.

Jesus was the perfect example of this. Some think He was sinless because He was 100% God. That's not the case, though, since He was 100% man, too. Hebrews 4:15 tells us that Jesus felt everything we felt and still did not sin. I'd imagine His temptation could have even been greater than ours since the enemy knew His purpose for being on the earth and was likely working overtime to stop Him. But as Isaiah 11:3 says, Jesus' delight was in fearing the Lord, and this kept Him on the Way. We see proof of this in Luke 22:44. Just before His crucifixion, Jesus prayed in the Garden of Gethsemane about what God would have Him do. He wanted to choose God's way so badly that He sweat blood! *That* is fear of the Lord.

The fear of the Lord was Jesus' anchor, and it can be ours, too. While those off the Way live with an unhealthy fear of others, we can live with a healthy fear of God. This will keep us grounded, walking the Way confidently, lighting a fire of love for Him in our hearts, and driving us to please Him. Scripture shows the rewards of living with the fear of the Lord.

In Isaiah 66:2b NASB, the prophet writes the Lord's declaration: "But I will look to this one, At one who is humble and contrite in spirit, and who trembles at My word." Our Maker is captivated by those who are humble, contrite in spirit, and tremble at His word because these are all signs of one who genuinely fears the Lord.

The psalmist writes about fearing the Lord in Psalm

25:12-15: "Who is the person who fears the Lord? He will instruct him in the way he should choose. His soul will dwell in prosperity, And his descendants will inherit the land. The secret of the Lord is for those who fear Him, And He will make them know His covenant. My eyes are continually toward the Lord, For He will rescue my feet from the net."

When we fear the Lord, God shines His favor on our life. He shares His secrets with us, and we gain a boldness for the journey unlike anything else. We can claim Hebrews 13:6 with confidence: "The Lord is my helper; I will not fear; what can man do to me?" When we prize fear for the Lord, we succeed on the Way. But when we don't, our trip could get cut short.

This is why, if I could only ask God for one thing for my children, it wouldn't be money or opportunity. It wouldn't be talent or gifting. I would pray that the fear of the Lord would arrest their hearts. Because the fear of the Lord is the beginning of wisdom, and this wisdom leads us to fall more in love with our Father, constantly pursuing His way. This Way alone will lead them into a beautiful, purpose-filled life better than they could've ever imagined.

ON THE ROAD AGAIN

As you've read through this chapter, you might have felt intense conviction. Perhaps you even sensed deep regret because you've given way to distraction, possibly even a detour. For some, that detour may have been brief, and for others, it may have taken years. No matter where you have found yourself, either in the past or present, understand this: you're in good company. Throughout history, *everyone* has proven unable to stay on the Way by their own power. Romans 3:23 confirms it: "...*all* have sinned and fall short of the glory of God." We *all* need His mercy, and it's vital to our future that we accept it.

Instead of getting stuck in guilt, defeat, or condemnation, we must remember: we are not a slave to the signs. We can accept God's mercy and let Him lead us back to the Way. Then, we can accept His grace to help us stay on the path.

The good news of Romans 8:35-39 reminds us that *nothing* can separate us from the love of Christ. *Nothing*. No matter how many exits we take, we cannot escape His love for us. We see this truth proven in the stories of the Israelites throughout the Old Testament. God had chosen the Israelites to walk His way, but they seemed to take every detour possible. As He always does, through the good, bad, and ugly, God continued to pursue them, beckoning them back to the Way. And when they came, He welcomed them with open arms.

> "We are not a slave to the signs. We can accept God's mercy and let Him lead us back to the Way."

We also see this truth proven in the story of Adam and Eve. After they committed the first sin on earth,

God found them, forgave them, pursued them, and invited them back to the Way. In doing so, He introduced His beautiful plan for redemption—not just for them, but for us, too. *All* of us. In the moments following their fall, God gave what we can consider the first gospel message. Here is what He said to the serpent: "Because you have done this, You are cursed more than all cattle, And more than every beast of the field; On your belly you shall go, And you shall eat dust All the days of your life. And I will put enmity Between you and the woman, And between your seed and her Seed; He shall bruise your head, And you shall bruise His heel" (Genesis 3:14-15).

> "Our Father has always had an answer, and His answer has always been Jesus."

The last part of this passage foreshadows God's plan of redemption through Jesus. Scholars often call Jesus "the second Adam," referring to the fact that Jesus came to redeem Adam's sin—to buy back the righteousness of all humanity. How amazing is our God? Before we ever took a detour—before we *ever* sinned—He already had a plan to redeem us, restore us, and get us back on His path again. Our Father has *always* had an answer, and His answer has *always* been Jesus. "But God demonstrates his own love for us in this: While we were still sinners, Christ died for us" (Romans 5:8 NIV).

This reality changes *everything*. When you started on the Way, you became an heir to the kingdom of God.

You are royalty! This is why Hebrews says you can boldly approach God's throne for mercy and grace to help
you in your time of need. If you ever find yourself on
another detour, you can confidently ask Him to redeem
and restore you, and
He will. Jesus will *al-
ways* be our redeem-
er and our rescuer.

"There are no bad days in
Jesus because there is no
greater news than the gospel."

He will *always* find us in whatever mess we've gotten
ourselves into and help us return to the right road again.
There are no bad days in Jesus because there is no greater news than the gospel.

> But the free gift is not like the offense. For if by
> the one man's offense many died, much more the
> grace of God and the gift by the grace of the one
> Man, Jesus Christ, abounded to many. And the
> gift is not like that which came through the one
> who sinned. For the judgment which came from
> one offense resulted in condemnation, but the
> free gift which came from many offenses result-
> ed in justification. For if by the one man's offense
> death reigned through the one, much more
> those who receive abundance of grace and of the
> gift of righteousness will reign in life through
> the One, Jesus Christ. Therefore, as through one
> man's offense judgment came to all men, result-
> ing in condemnation, even so through one Man's

righteous act the free gift came to all men, resulting in justification of life. For as by one man's disobedience many were made sinners, so also by one Man's obedience many will be made righteous (Romans 5:15-19).

Where are you today? Are you confidently making progress on the Way? Are you off-road but want to get back on? If the latter is where you are, and you desire God's redemption and restoration in your life, I invite you to pray this with me:

God,

I am sorry for submitting to the enemy's distractions. I want to live your way. Please help me get back on your path. When I'm there, continue to enlarge my heart and give me the grace to walk your way. Thank you for your mercy.

In Jesus' name, Amen.

From this day forward, remember: you are no longer a slave to the signs. You're redeemed and justified, so in God's eyes, it's as if you never took a detour to begin with. As you continue on the Way, allowing God to enlarge your heart consistently, these detours will appear less enticing. You'll enjoy the progress you make *today* as you consistently sow seed for a better *tomorrow*.

CHAPTER SIX

SOW AND SEE

I**T'S A SCIENTIFIC** reality: what you sow, you'll eventually see. What you plant will produce when the harvest time comes. It is not just a physical reality; it's a spiritual one, too. "Do not be deceived: God is not mocked, for whatever one sows, that will he also reap. For the one who sows into his own flesh will reap from the flesh corruption, but the one who sows to the Spirit will from the Spirit reap eternal life" (Galatians 6:7-8 ESV).

This is a pillar of truth Abby and I held on to upon graduating from Bible school. I knew I was called to pastor. God had spoken clearly to me, and I had done my best to prepare myself. But in my immaturity, I assumed that a job would be waiting for me as soon as I graduated.

Since that wasn't the reality, I took a minimum-wage

job as a courier to make ends meet. During this time, I learned many invaluable lessons, one of the most important being this: in the dry seasons, we must be careful what we plant. Why? Because we can't see evidence of what we planted yet. We likely won't see the fruit of our decisions for a while, but don't be fooled—the seed *is* taking root and the harvest *is* on the way.

Thank God my wife understood this principle. During those early days, I would often wake up to encouragement on post-it notes strategically placed all over our home. I would find my suitcases laid out with a sign that read, "Matthew Pollock: the nations' preacher." In that season, her faith inspired me to plant my own seeds. I packed my duffle bag with my Amplified Bible, ESV Bible, and Strong's Concordance. On my lunch break, when everyone else was eating, I would set up a makeshift office and study the Word for an hour. I sowed in the dry season what I wanted to see at harvest time.

Those moments are precious to me because they laid the foundation for the work I do today. I am also grateful for what they meant to my coworkers' lives. That consistent sowing caught many of their attention, and I received the honor of leading some of them to Jesus.

During the dry seasons, don't allow discouragement to derail you because how you handle those days will affect the days to come. They'll also speak more loudly to those around you than you might realize. So find purpose in every moment and keep sowing what you want to see.

Psalm 119:31 reminds us that when we cling to God's testimonies—His Word—we will never be put to shame. Instead, that Word will drown out trauma and insecurity as God expands our hearts so that we can hold onto His promise until it is fulfilled. It's not easy, though. It's an investment of both time and effort. You've got to sow even when you don't feel like it—even when the harvest seems slow, and your present reality makes it seem unattainable.

The truth is that the Word takes work, and the apostle Paul understood the consistent effort it requires. That's why, after encouraging us about sowing and reaping, in the very next verse, he addresses the dry seasons. "And let us not grow weary of doing good, for in due season we will reap, if we do not give up" (Galatians 6:9 ESV). If we continue to sow the Word of God into our spirits, we will reap growth, fruitfulness, and maturity, allowing us to walk into the incredible futures God has for us.

When we bought our first home, Abby again put this truth into action. She wanted a verse to stand on for our children, so she sought the Lord for one. Then, she went to Hobby Lobby, bought stencils, and prophetically wrote that verse on the walls of their rooms. The word was *literally* all over our home because Abby understood the importance of sowing into our children in the "dry season" when we probably wouldn't see much of the fruit of our labor. Now that our kids are nearly grown, we have experienced a beautiful harvest. In your family and in your life, the Word will take work. Trust me, though: the payoff will be more than worth it.

> You shall therefore lay up these words of mine in your heart and in your soul, and you shall bind them as a sign on your hand, and they shall be frontlets between your eyes. You shall teach them to your children, talking of them when you are sitting in your house, and when you are walking by the way, and when you lie down, and when you rise. You shall write them on the doorposts of your house and on your gates, that your days and the days of your children may be multiplied in the land that the Lord swore to your fathers to give them, as long as the heavens are above the earth (Deuteronomy 11:18-21 ESV).

Now, before we continue further, I encourage you to reflect. What are you sowing into your future? What are you sowing into your children's futures? Are you constantly speaking of your worries, or are you speaking God's Word? Are you listening to music and podcasts that build your faith? Or are your media choices distracting you from the Way? When we hide the Word in our hearts, it will be there when we need it most.

One of my favorite things about consistently sowing

the Word in our hearts is the boldness it produces. It's not just any boldness, though. It's the kind that helped a shepherd boy kill a giant and a stuttering murderer lead a people. We see a prime example of this boldness in the story of Shammah, which Scripture lists as one of King David's mighty warriors. Here is the description: "And next to him was Shammah, the son of Agee the Hararite. The Philistines gathered together at Lehi, where there was a plot of ground full of lentils, and the men fled from the Philistines. But he took his stand in the midst of the plot and defended it and struck down the Philistines, and the Lord worked a great victory" (2 Samuel 23:11-12).

> "Do the work of the word throughout each season, and it will produce boldness for every battle."

I encourage you not to underestimate what the Lord has given you. Defend it. Protect it against all odds. For Shammah, it was a pea patch. For you, it could be a dream, a word from God, or your family. Whether you stand on a stage or sit in a conference room, trade stocks or pack lunches—wherever you spend your days, protect your ground. Do the work of the Word throughout each season, and it will produce boldness for every battle.

ABIDING

Doing the work of the word is called something else throughout Scripture: abiding. "As he was saying these things, many believed in him. So Jesus said to the Jews who had believed him, "If you *abide* in my word, you are truly my disciples, and you will know the truth, and the truth will set you free" (John 8:31-32 ESV).

This passage gives us the last step we'll take along our journey on the Way. We've already discerned the hour we're in and decided the path we will take. We applied the truth when we started walking. Now, we have to abide. To abide is to dwell, stay, or continue. You could actually interchange the words "abide" and "continue" in this passage based on the language Jesus spoke it in. When we *continue* in the truth, it becomes a reality in our lives.

This final point is where many people give up. Sure, they may go to church regularly. They might hear the new worship song and feel goosebumps when it's sung. They may even leave inspired by the message. But that's where it stops. Their heart doesn't enlarge, and their life doesn't change. Why? Because when they leave church, their Bible stays closed, and everything else gets their attention.

> "When we *continue* in the truth, it becomes a reality in our lives."

We will always be a byproduct of what we abide in. We will always see what we sow and eat the fruit of the seed we plant. It's like working out. I can say I want to be fit, but if I hired a personal trainer, my desire would be tested. The trainer might tell me, "Be at the gym at 6 a.m. every day this year. Cut out all sugar. Lower your carbs." If I abided by these instructions, I would reap the fruit I desired. If I gave up after two weeks and began abiding in my bed and donuts instead, I would reap the opposite.

It's easy to desire the result but give up before we get it. Along our journey on the Way, it's the same. We want the signs, the miracles, and the anoint-

> "We will always be a byproduct of what we abide in."

ing, but will we do the work of the Word? It's *only* abiding in the Word—His truth—that sets us free. Jesus further proves the importance of abiding with these words: "And it happened, as He spoke these things, that a certain woman from the crowd raised her voice and said to Him, 'Blessed is the womb that bore You, and the breasts which nursed You!' But He said, 'More than that, blessed are those who hear the word of God and keep it'" (Luke 11:27-28)!

I'm sure this response shocked people, but Jesus wanted to clarify that obediently abiding in the Word is a big deal to God. It's why we can't just observe it; we must also obey it. We can't just hear it; we must also heed it. We must continually subject our lives to it, building upon its foundation and allowing it to have ultimate authority in our lives. Yes, it will take discipline. Yes, it will take energy. That's why the psalmist wrote in Psalm 119:32 that he *runs* in the ways of God's commandments.

The Word takes work, and abiding takes effort.

We're all expending energy daily on things that matter to us. So where is yours going? When we run in the way of worry, it uses the energy we need to run after God. When we run in the way of fear, gossip, or striving, it uses the energy we need to abide. When we continue in God's Word, however, making progress along the Way, we receive deep personal revelation. We experience an intimate relationship unlike any that we've ever had. It's truly transformational.

One of my favorite things about this process is that it often takes only one word from God to change your life. Sometimes, God will give this to you as a word of knowledge, but many times, He'll speak to you through the words of Scripture. The latter is the predominant way He speaks to me. When our congregation was believing for a building to gather in, the Lord led me to these words: "For the Lord has chosen Zion; he has desired it for his dwelling place: 'This is my resting place forever; here I will dwell, for I have desired it. I will abundantly bless her provisions; I will satisfy her poor with bread. Her priests I will clothe with salvation, and her saints will shout for joy'" (Psalm 132:13-16 ESV).

While reading this passage, the Lord impressed upon me that He had chosen a "Zion" for us—a physical location where we could gather to worship. He said that He would bless us there, and He did. It wasn't easy, though. The Word took work. We had to abide by it daily, focusing on what the Lord had spoken. We had to guard our pea patch against every effort of the enemy, relying on the boldness that came from doing the work of the Word.

For what problem do you need a promise? I encourage you to spend time in God's Word. Get a personal revelation, and then abide in that word. Hold it with a firm grip, never letting it go. If you do, you'll see that promise fulfilled. It probably won't be easy, but you'll be glad you held on.

Now that we know the final stage of our journey on the Way, let's reflect on how to abide. Though there are many keys, these five have helped me stay committed when everything in me wants to veer.

INTEGRATION

The first key to abiding is integration. In today's fast-paced culture, we all wear many hats. We've got our God hat, our career hat, our social hat, our family hat, and the list goes on. Because of this, we often compartmentalize the truth based on what hat we're wearing. We might use God's truth at church, but what about in our social compartment? Maybe we feel we have it figured out, so we don't submit as much. Or maybe we trust what God says about marriage, but the truth as it relates to our finances? We skip that.

This isn't how it should be. When we are *really* abiding in truth, that truth will invade *everything* we do and *everything* we are. Only when we integrate the truth into every area of our lives—fully yielding to it—can we abide.

HUMILITY

Another major key is humility, a topic found throughout Proverbs. "The fear of the Lord is hatred of evil. Pride and arrogance and the way of evil and perverted speech I hate" (Proverbs 8:13 ESV). God hates pride because it prevents progress and keeps us from Him.

The truth is simple: the more humble we are, the greater God can move in our lives, and the more prideful we are, the less He can move. God *wants* to do great things in and through us, but we must first embrace humility, opening our hearts to the work of the Word. When we do, it naturally leads to our next key: submission.

SUBMISSION

God is a God of order, and He set this order before time, giving us each a place. His place is first in everything. To abide in Christ, all we are and all we have must fall under God's authority. He doesn't require this for His sake, though; He requires it for our sake. He knows living under His authority is safe, and it will cause us to win every time. So, let's not waste time. Let's do things God's way now.

Do you need help with parenting? Financial management? Time management? Marriage? Work? The answers are *all* in His Word. When you submit to His ways, you find success. So get in the Word, and do what God says. Then, you'll receive what He has promised.

UNITY

The next step happens naturally when we continually submit ourselves to God's processes. We begin operating in unity with Him. It's like marriage. When I said yes to Abby, I committed to a life of oneness with her. That means I'm not just married to her at home; I'm married to her everywhere I go. It's the same with God. When we continually say yes to His way, His character takes root in us. His Word *becomes* who we are. It allows our born-again nature to take over.

There can be no newness of life unless dying happens first. "We were buried therefore with him by baptism unto death, in order that, just as Christ was raised from the dead by the glory of the Father, we too might walk in newness of life" (Romans 6:4 ESV). When we live in true unity with Christ, we live differently, and this new way of living helps us continue faithfully on our journey.

UNDERSTANDING

The final key I'll leave you with is understanding. This is a big one because you'll have to use it often along the Way. You won't have to walk far before you realize that here, just as everywhere else, no one is perfect. Christians, churches, and pastors will fail you, but when they do, you must remember that your future lies not in what they do to you but in how you respond. Will you choose offense? Or will you choose understanding? To abide, we *must* choose understanding. We *must* live with compassion when others miss the mark, forgiving them quickly and fully.

Jesus gave us the golden rule in Luke 6:31, and in the verses that follow, He clarifies it further. He wants us to know we're not just to love, forgive, and do good to our circle of friends. He wants us to love, forgive, and do good to *all* people—even our enemies.

> If you love those who love you, what benefit is that to you? For even sinners love those who love them. And if you do good to those who do good to you, what benefit is that to you? For even sinners do the same. And if you lend to those from whom you expect to receive, what credit is that to you? Even sinners lend to sinners, to get back the same amount. But love your enemies, and do good, and lend, expecting nothing in return, and your reward will be great, and you will be sons of the Most High, for he is kind to the ungrateful and the evil. Be merciful, even as your Father is merciful (Luke 6:32-36 ESV).

In the abiding stage of your journey, there will still be times you'll be tempted to exit. When this happens, stop and pray. Ask God what area might be lacking. Then make the necessary adjustments to get back to abiding. We make consistent progress along the Way of Truth when we truly embrace integration, humility, submission, unity, and understanding. And the last one—understanding—is crucial to keeping us firmly planted in the Place of Truth—the local church.

CHAPTER SEVEN

THE PLACE OF TRUTH

PLACES ARE IMPORTANT to God, and they always have been. We see this when Jesus talked to the disciples about the places He was preparing for us in heaven. "In my Father's house are many rooms. If it were not so, would I have told you that I go to prepare a place for you? And if I go and prepare a place for you, I will come again and will take you to myself, that where I am you may be also" (John 14:2-3 ESV).

Places aren't just important, though; they're also specific, and they play a specific role in God's purposes for us. If we don't show up to these places, we can miss out in big ways. We see this truth play out in Scripture. In 1 Corinthians 15, we learn that Jesus told more than

500 people to gather in the upper room at Pentecost, but in Acts, we see that only 120 did. The 120 believers filled with the Holy Spirit that day eventually changed the world, but can you imagine what would have happened if the other 380-plus people had been there, too?

We see this same truth made evident in the story of Elijah, the prophet, who declared a coming drought. When that drought came, God told him, "Depart eastward and hide yourself by the brook Cherith, which is east of the Jordan. You shall drink from the brook, and I have commanded the ravens to feed you there. So he went and did according to the word of the lord. He went and lived by the brook Cherish that is east of the Jordan" (1 Kings 17:3-5 ESV).

Elijah did what the Lord told him. He traveled to the specific place God instructed, and because of his obedience, God provided, even when it made little sense. God used ravens to bring Elijah food, which was unusual since ravens are known for taking—not giving. Perhaps God was reminding Elijah (and us!) that if we honor the places He has called us to, He will provide, even when things look impossible. He will cause our finances to thrive in a terrible economy, our health to improve after a negative report, and our relationships to mend after a death sentence. But we have to be at the brook. We must get to the upper room. We've got to show up at the place He wants us to receive His supernatural provision.

Another story that proves the importance of places

is the Apostle Paul's conversion in Acts 9. At this time, Paul was called *Saul* and was known for persecuting Christians. While on his way to Damascus to continue his work, the Lord got his attention.

> Now as he went on his way, he approached Damascus, and suddenly a light from heaven shone around him. And falling to the ground, he heard a voice saying to him, "Saul, Saul, why are you persecuting me?" And he said, "Who are you, Lord?" And he said, "I am Jesus, whom you are persecuting. But rise and enter the city, and you will be told what you are to do." The men who were traveling with him stood speechless, hearing the voice but seeing no one. Saul rose from the ground, and although his eyes were opened, he saw nothing. So they led him by the hand and brought him into Damascus. And for three days he was without sight, and neither ate nor drank (Acts 9:3-9 ESV).

Obviously, Jesus could have healed Saul immediately after speaking to him, but He didn't. Instead, He directed him to a place to receive his healing. He also instructed Ananias to go to the same place at the same time so that he could pray for Saul. When both men obeyed and showed up, a miracle happened. Paul received his sight, and he lived the rest of his life building the kingdom of God.

Like Paul, Elijah, and the witnesses in the upper room, along our journey on the Way of Truth, we'll all have specific places God calls us to, and it's vital that we show up. But there is also one place we all share, and it's the most important one we could ever say yes to. It's God's address here on earth. It's the Place of Truth—the local church. This doesn't mean we all attend the same physical gathering, of course, because though the church is one body, it assembles in many locations worldwide. Paul spoke of the importance of the local church in one of his letters to his spiritual son, Timothy, who was working in the church in Ephesus.

> These things I write to you, though I hope to come to you shortly; but if I am delayed, I write so that you may know how you ought to conduct yourself in the house of God, which is the church of the living God, the pillar and ground of the truth. And without controversy great is the mystery of godliness:
>
> God was manifested in the flesh,
> Justified in the Spirit,
> Seen by angels,
> Preached among the Gentiles,
> Believed on in the world,
> Received up in glory (1 Timothy 3:14-16).

Here, Paul calls the church a pillar and ground of

truth, proving that it is absolutely necessary to the life of every believer because of the "mystery of godliness" it solves for us. It's in the church that we learn God's truth and how to walk in it.

Like Paul, many of us met God on a road we weren't proud of walking. And as He did with Paul, God redeemed us and then presented us with a choice. We can choose to stay where we're at, blinded to the miracles in our future. Or we can obey and get ourselves to the place He is calling us to—the local church. There, we will experience miracles and gain a fresh vision for our lives.

OUT, TO, IN

As you read Paul's letters throughout the New Testament, it's hard to believe he ever worked against the church. His passion for it is so strong! He wrote many letters encouraging, rebuking, and teaching the church in its infancy. In his original language, Greek, the word for the church is *Ekklēsia*, defined by *The Encyclopedia Britannica* as a "gathering of those summoned."[15] So throughout his letters, he encourages believers to approach Jesus' summoning in three ways.

The first key Paul teaches is that the church is *called out*—to live set apart. "Do not be unequally yoked together with unbelievers. For what fellowship has righteousness with lawlessness? And what communion has light with darkness?...'Therefore come out from among them and be separate'" (2 Corinthians 6:14, 17).

Many think they can have both the Way and the world, but that's not how it works. Once you've decided to commit to Jesus, you are changed forever. We live *in* the world, but we'll never fit into it because we've been made divinely distinct. We're now royalty.

The second piece of wisdom Paul gives is that God wants His church to be *called to* covenant. As walkers of the Way, we're called to a forever relationship with Christ, one we never abandon. The third thing Paul encourages us is that we should be *called in*. We should be part of a local body of believers.

This last one is where many have trouble. While they have chosen the Way and a covenant relationship with their Father, they don't understand the value of the Place of Truth. Maybe they feel it's unnecessary because of the plethora of anointed messages and powerful worship music on YouTube. Maybe they're too busy, or they can't find a place that feels like home. Perhaps they've even endured hurt at the hands of the church. While I certainly don't make light of this, trust me, the answer is never to give up on the place because of the people.

Charles Spurgeon once said, "The church is not perfect, but woe to the man who finds pleasure in pointing out Her imperfections!"[16] We are *all* imperfect people serving a perfect God and striving to make His perfect love known to all. Yes, we fall short, and sometimes, in extremely disappointing ways. But let's not give up on a perfect God because of imperfect people. That's exactly what our enemy wants.

See, the enemy knows how vital the church is, so he works overtime to keep us from it. Remember the statistics in our first chapter? He knows if he can offend us, push us into apathy, or hinder us from planting ourselves in a local church, we'll eventually exit off the Way. He knows it's in the Place of Truth that we develop relationships with other believers who will help us stay committed to the path. And more importantly, He knows Jesus is there.

> "Never give up on a perfect God because of imperfect people. That's exactly what our enemy wants."

For by him all things were created, in heaven and on earth, visible and invisible, whether thrones or dominions or rulers or authorities—all things were created through him and for him. And he is before all things, and in him all things hold together. And he is the head of the body, the church. He is the beginning, the first-born from the dead, that in everything he might be pre-eminent. For in him all the fullness of God was pleased to dwell, and through him to reconcile to himself all things, whether on earth or in heaven, making peace by the blood of his cross (Colossians 1:16-20 ESV).

It's impossible to separate Jesus from His church. He will always be there, and this reality will always make the church the most important place on earth. Here we can reach up, exalting the Lord, reach down, declaring our victory over the enemy, and reach out, spreading the gospel message of hope to those around us.

A GREAT RESPONSIBILITY

Solomon lived well before the establishment of the first church, but he still understood its importance. He knew that every city needed a Place of Truth where they could learn God's principles that would enlarge their hearts and transform their lives. Because of this, God trusted him to build His first physical house on earth—the first temple.

Solomon knew that serving as king of God's people was an enormous responsibility. So in prayer, he sought God for wisdom. First Kings 3:5 (ESV) says, "At Gibeon, the Lord appeared to Solomon in a dream by night, and God said, 'Ask what I shall give you.'" Solomon asked for wisdom and understanding, and Scripture says this request moved God's heart. It impressed Him that Solomon didn't ask for wealth, riches, or fame—he asked for *wisdom*. Because of this, God blessed Solomon with more than just wisdom. Not only did he become the wisest person on earth, but he also became the wealthiest.

God visited Solomon again after he had finished building the temple and gathered the people to dedicate it to the Lord.

> And it came to pass, when Solomon had finished building the house of the Lord and the king's house, and all Solomon's desire which he wanted to do, that the Lord appeared to Solomon

the second time, as He had appeared to him at Gibeon. And the Lord said to him: "I have heard your prayer and your supplication that you have made before Me; I have consecrated this house which you have built to put My name there forever, and My eyes and My heart will be there perpetually" (I Kings 9: 1-3).

Here, God promised Solomon three things regarding the temple, and He makes these three promises to our churches today. First, He promises His name, meaning He will live there forever. It will be His house, where people can come to encounter Him. Then, He promises His eyes, committing to giving them His constant and full attention. Lastly, He marks it with His heart, which means He gives the church His deepest affection.

It's clear from this passage alone how special our churches are to the heart of God. Solomon recognized it, and we must, too. Then, like Solomon, we must go from *recognizing* it to taking *responsibility* for it. Of course, this may not be in a physical sense. We might never personally build a physical location where God dwells, but we are all called to build His church by showing up, worshiping, learning, serving, giving, and inviting others to join us.

The unfortunate problem is that many people, likely with good hearts, so desperately want to build something for God that they try to build on their own rather than being a part of something He is already building. Bono, singer-songwriter and walker of the Way talked about this in his keynote address at the 54th National Prayer Breakfast in 2006.

A number of years ago, I met a wise man who changed my life in countless ways, big and small. I was always seeking the Lord's blessing. I'd be saying, "Look, I've got a new song… Would you look out [for it]? I have a family; I'm going away on tour. Please look after them. I have this crazy idea. Could I have a blessing on it?" And this wise man asked me to stop. He said, "Stop asking God to bless what you're doing. Get involved in what God is doing because it's already blessed."[17]

The enemy knows we are much more powerful together, so he will do everything he can to keep us apart. If we want God's church to thrive in an hour it is arguably the most needed on the earth, we must show up. We have to serve, love, give, and witness well. Above all else, we have to say yes to Jesus, adopting *His* standard of loving the church.

A HOLY STANDARD

Jesus set this standard for us when He walked the earth. He taught us to honor, cherish, and protect God's house and to live in a way that attracts believers to it. In Luke 2, we get a glimpse of His love for God's house, even as a child.

Scholars say Jesus was about 12 years old at this time.

It was Passover, so He and His family followed tradition, traveling to Jerusalem for the feasts. After their time there was over, Jesus' parents left. They had traveled a full day by the time they realized Jesus was missing. Of course, they panicked. They searched everywhere until they finally found Him.

> After three days they found him in the temple, sitting among the teachers, listening to them and asking them questions. And all who heard him were amazed at his understanding and his answers. And when his parents saw him, they were astonished. And his mother said to him, "Son, why have you treated us so? Behold, your father and I have been searching for you in great distress." And he said to them, "Why were you looking for me? Did you not know that I must be in my Father's house?" (Luke 2:46-49 ESV)

Jesus longed to be in His Father's house, and as He grew, that love did, too. He both began and ended His earthly ministry by caring for the temple. In John 2:13-22, just after He had performed His first miracle of turning water into wine, Jesus cleansed the temple. He drove everything out of it that was not in line with God's heart, fulfilling the prophecy in Psalm 69:9 ESV that says, "For zeal for your house has consumed me." About three years later, in Matthew 21:12-17, He did the same thing again.

Jesus didn't purge the temple to be harsh. That's not His nature. He did it to remind us that, as the church, we are called to this higher standard of loving God, His house, and His people. Our lives were meant to serve as an example to unbelievers, attracting them to join us in our churches and, ultimately, on the Way.

God needs *you* to be His standard on earth. He needs you to zealously love His church, even when it's hard. He needs you to passionately love others, even when they fall short. He needs you to live wholeheartedly as His child, set apart for Him.

> "Keeping God's standard—living as His children—is the honor of our lives."

Though it's not always easy, the longer we walk on the Way of Truth, the more we realize what Jesus knew: keeping God's standard—living as His children—is the honor of our lives.

THE CHURCH IS ALIVE

So now, we've discussed the importance of the Place of Truth. We know we've got to show up—to live called *out* of the world, *to* Christ, and *in* a local body of believers. We also know that we are responsible for building the kingdom of God by setting the standard for others that beckons them to join us. Now, I want to remind you of a simple truth. God's church is not dead. It's as alive as He is.

Jesus makes this clear in Matthew 16. Peter (then

known as Simon) was with Him and other disciples at a place called Caesarea Philippi, once marked as the access point of hell on the earth. Jesus asked His disciples, "Who do you say I am?" Peter replied, "You are the Messiah, the Son of the Living God."

> "Blessed are you, Simon Bar-Jonah, for flesh and blood has not revealed this to you, but My Father who is in heaven. And I also say to you that you are Peter, and on this rock I will build My church, and the gates of Hades shall not prevail against it. And I will give you the keys of the kingdom of heaven, and whatever you bind on earth will be bound in heaven, and whatever you loose on earth will be loosed in heaven" (Matthew 16:17-19 ESV).

No matter what any news article, statistic, or person tells you, our God is alive, and so is His church. Just as Christ loves, protects, and honors His church and just as He lived in a way that drew others in, let us always and forever do the same.

CHAPTER EIGHT

THE FAITHFUL CHURCH

WHEN YOU HEAR the word "church," it likely elicits some type of response. You could feel grateful, shameful, hopeful, or hurt. We all have various ways of viewing the church based on our experiences. But to rightly receive from the Place of Truth, we must see it with an accurate perspective—God's.

To understand God's perspective of and plan for His church, we must first recognize its vital place not just in our lives but also in our society. As we mentioned in the last chapter, it is a pillar, the ground of truth, and the firmest foundation. It is the bedrock of our culture, upholding every other positive structure. If we remove the church, everything else crumbles—marriages, families, businesses, *everything*.

Satan knows better than anyone that as the church goes, the city goes, and as the city goes, the nation goes. It is why he has worked incessantly to discredit and disband the church in each generation. He knows he can't ultimately beat the church, so he comes after your perspective of it. He realizes that if he can get you to see the church differently than God does, you'll never receive the truth He offers.

That's what I want us to unpack in this chapter. I want us to explore Scripture together, discovering how God views His church. As you read, compare His view to yours. Find discrepancies in your perspective and ask God to help you see things differently. As we open our hearts and minds to His perspective, I believe a passion for the church He built will develop, re-develop, or strengthen our hearts.

A PORTAL

In Genesis, we're given a prophetic picture of one way God sees His church—as a portal, the point at which heaven gains access to our cities. We see this through Jacob's dream.

> And he dreamed, and behold, there was a ladder set up on the earth, and the top of it reached to heaven. And behold, the angels of God were ascending and descending on it! And behold, the Lord stood above it and said, "I am the Lord,

the God of Abraham your father and the God of Isaac. The land on which you lie I will give to you and to your offspring. Your offspring shall be like the dust of the earth, and you shall spread abroad to the west and to the east and to the north and to the south, and in you and your offspring shall all the families of the earth be blessed. Behold, I am with you and will keep you wherever you go, and will bring you back to this land. For I will not leave you until I have done what I have promised you." Then Jacob awoke from his sleep and said, "Surely the Lord is in this place, and I did not know it." And he was afraid and said, "How awesome is this place! This is none other than the house of God, and this is the gate of heaven" (Genesis 28:12-17 ESV).

The house of God is the gate of heaven, and Jesus is the ladder that provides access to it. When we come together to worship our Father, it gives Him a point of access into our cities, states, and nation so that

> "As the church goes, the city goes, and as the city goes, the nation goes."

He can touch hearts and transform the earth. Verses 18-22 ESV continue with Jacob's response:

So early in the morning Jacob took the stone that he had put under his head and set it up for a pillar and poured oil on the top of it. He called the name of that place Bethel, but the name of the city was Luz at the first. Then Jacob made a vow, saying, "If God will be with me and will keep me in this way that I go, and will give me bread to eat and clothing to wear, so that I come again to my father's house in peace, then the Lord shall be my God, and this stone, which I have set up for a pillar, shall be God's house. And of all that you give me I will give a full tenth to you."

When Jacob awakened from his sleep, he awakened with a reverent fear for God's house. I like how the Message translation puts his response. It says, "Jacob woke up from his sleep. He said, 'God is in this place—truly. And I didn't even know it!' He was terrified. He whispered in awe, 'Incredible. Wonderful. Holy. This is God's house. This is the Gate of Heaven (16, 17).'" But Jacob didn't stop with awe; he put that awe into action. He made a vow to the Lord to prioritize His house. When we see God's house as the access point of heaven, we will respond like Jacob did—with reverence, awe, and commitment.

A HOUSEHOLD

Another way God sees His church is as His house—a household of faith. God is our Father, and everything He does is family focused. Paul confirms this perspective with these words: "So then, as we have the opportunity, let us do good to everyone, and especially to those who are of the household of faith" (Galatians 6:10 ESV).

When we gather, it's like a big family meeting, and just like in a family meeting, I believe the Father takes attendance. He accepts our worship as we are, but He also judges the sincerity of our hearts. God measures how well we honor Him, how lovingly we serve others, and how willingly we invest in His house. God watches how we contribute to the family and deals with any problems that arise. His heart is for His household to remain strong, vibrant, and effective.

In a healthy family, we're offered a strong sense of safety and protection. That's what the church should be to us, too. We see this truth prophetically outlined in the story of Noah. When God spoke to Noah to build the ark, no one had ever seen rain. Still, he listened to God's instruction as described in these words: "By faith Noah, being divinely warned of things not yet seen, moved with godly fear, prepared an ark for the saving of his household, by which he condemned the world and became heir of the righteousness which is according to faith" (Hebrews 11:7).

Like Noah, if we work together to build the church during our sunnier seasons, it'll be our safe place in the stormy ones, too. It will be a place of refuge for our families and for us.

A BRIDE

One of the most popular names Scripture gives the church is the bride. The church and marriage are the only two institutions God created, reflecting the greatest love we'll ever know on this side of heaven. The church is a sacred, special gift of God—a parable of the union between a man and woman. Just as in a marriage, a man is to be one with a woman, so the church is to be one with Christ, in perfect unity with His Spirit. And just like in a godly marriage a man and woman are to remain committed to each other "until death do us part," we are to remain committed to Christ to the end.

A FLOCK

In the Book of Acts, we find another name Scripture gives the church—a flock.

> Therefore take heed to yourselves and to all the flock, among which the Holy Spirit has made you overseers, to shepherd the church of God which He purchased with His own blood. For I know this, that after my departure savage wolves will come in among you, not sparing the flock (Acts 20:28-29).

In Jesus' day, a father handling his household affairs would assign one of his sons to shepherd his flock. That's what God does with His church. He assigns pastors to churches and charges them with oversight of

His sheep's journey on the Way. When the enemy, like wolves, comes to sabotage our journey, distort God's message, and hurt the church, the pastor is called to protect us.

This perspective could dramatically alter how we view the church if we let it. Here's how: if you've trusted God to lead you to the local church He has picked out for you, then you should trust that God has specifically chosen your pastor to care for you and your family, just as He would trust a shepherd with sheep. Will your pastor be perfect? No. No one is perfect. But if you follow God's leading, you can trust you will receive all you need from being a part of that flock.

> "In a world where it seems many could take or leave the Church, God has not thrown us aside."

Thank God, in a world where it seems many could take or leave the church, God has not thrown us aside. He sent His Son to purchase us with His precious blood. Like sheep to a shepherd, we are invaluable to Him!

AN ASSEMBLY

Another common name given to the church throughout the New Testament is an assembly or a body. God uses this perspective to show us that, like a body is one with many parts, so is the church one body with many members. We all have a part to play in building God's kingdom. Without us, the picture is unfinished; with us, it's complete.

It's like a Lego set. One piece sitting by itself makes nothing great, but when you put all the pieces together, each serving its appropriate function, something beautiful is created. It's the same in the church. On our own, we're limited in what we can do. However, when we work together, each serving in the space God has called us to, we build something bigger and more beautiful than anything we could have created on our own. Paul gives us insight into this in his letter to the church in Ephesus.

> And He Himself gave some to be apostles, some prophets, some evangelists, and some pastors and teachers, for the equipping of the saints for the work of ministry, for the edifying of the body of Christ, till we all come to the unity of the faith and of the knowledge of the Son of God, to a perfect man, to the measure of the stature of the fullness of Christ; that we should no longer be children, tossed to and fro and carried about with every wind of doctrine, by the trickery of men, in the cunning craftiness of deceitful plotting, but, speaking the truth in love, may grow up in all things into Him who is the head—Christ— from whom the whole body, joined and knit together by what every joint supplies, according to the effective working by which every part does its share, causes growth of the body for the edifying of itself in love (Ephesians 4:11-16).

God has called none of us to be lone rangers, walking the Way of Truth alone. You have what I need; I have what you need. Each of our gifts is crucial for the church to fulfill what God has called us to do. Assembly is *always* required because there is strength in union. "And let us consider one another in order to stir up love and good works, not forsaking the assembling of ourselves together, as is the manner of some, but exhorting one another, and so much the more as you see the Day approaching" (Hebrews 10:24-25).

Ignatius said, "When you frequently, and in numbers, meet together, the powers of Satan are overthrown, and his mischief is neutralized by your like-mindedness in the faith."[18] We cannot give up on assembling in the house of God. It is a spiritual, biblical duty that God has commanded. He didn't just command it for the good of the church, though; He commanded it for the benefit of our souls. Gathering with believers is essential for our spiritual well-being and growth. When we neglect it, we starve our souls and spiritually bankrupt our lives.

A BASE

In 1 Timothy 3:14-16, which we discussed in the last chapter, Paul calls the church a pillar. In Greek, the original language in which this text was written, the word Paul uses for *pillar* offers a unique perspective on how God views His church. It compares it to a military base.

A military base is a facility directly owned and operated by and for the military or one of its branches. Military equipment, personnel, faculties, and training operations are located there. It serves as a command center, where people receive the intelligence they need to accomplish their mission. It also serves as a training ground, where troops become equipped to carry out orders.

The church is our spiritual military base. It's our command center, where we receive heaven's intelligence, and our training ground, where we become equipped to fight well. Just as a military cannot function without its base, a believer cannot function without their local church. Unfortunately, many try, and they end up in midair without artillery. Before we ever enter the fight of our daily lives, it's vital that we first report to the base to receive our orders and to get the intelligence and weapons we need to experience victory.

AN HONOR

We've covered many ways God presents the church to His people in Scripture, but one trumps them all: honor. Being a part of the church is the greatest privilege of our lives. It's a beautiful benefit for every believer to worship, hear the Word, and serve. Who are we that God would allow us to be kings and priests in His house? Who are we that He has entrusted us to give to our local church to help build His kingdom? No matter how busy we get, we must never diminish the profound honor of simply *being* the church where Christ rules.

"At the center of all this, Christ rules the church. The church, you see, is not peripheral to the world; the world is peripheral to the church. The church is Christ's body, in which he speaks and acts, by which he fills everything with his presence (Ephesians 1:22-23 MSG). The church is second to none. It has always been and will always be irreplaceable. If it is the foundation for every other positive establishment in our lives, shouldn't we give it our utmost attention? Shouldn't we make it our priority?

In chapter one, we mentioned the seven churches Jesus judged in the last days. There were two that received no rebuke. One of these—the sixth church—is the church of Philadelphia. I believe this church should be our goal at this hour. The church of Philadelphia wasn't large. They didn't have wealth, fame, or notoriety, but they didn't play the victim, begging for more. Instead, they protected what they had been given. They treasured the house of God.

In Revelation 3:7-13, we read about this church, which the author calls "the faithful church." In verse 10, Jesus affirms the churches' steadfastness to keep His Word and leaves them with a promise. "Because you have kept My command to persevere, I also will keep you from the hour of trial which shall come upon the whole world, to test those who dwell on the earth."

I often wonder—how will the Lord find *us* when He returns? Will we be like the church of Philadelphia? Will we fully commit to loving His name, His house, and His people? Will we stay pure, persevering to the end?

Several times throughout Scripture, including in 1 Corinthians 16:22 and Revelation 22:12, writers use the word *Maranatha,* meaning "Come, our Lord!" This word expresses both their anticipation and excitement about the return of Jesus. Can we boldly declare the same with confidence, knowing that we have remained fully committed to His Way of Truth and Place of Truth? Or will we allow ourselves to focus on peoples' imperfections to the point of stagnancy?

The church is not perfect. It never has been and never will be. But if we adopt God's perspective of it, as Jesus did, we will grow in love for our Father's house every day. When we fall more in love with the Place of Truth, we will receive all we need to keep walking on the Way of Truth. Like the church of Philadelphia, we will find the grace to remain faithful to the end, declaring with passionate excitement and conviction, "Come, our Lord! Come!"

CHAPTER NINE

TO THE END

THE ESV TRANSLATION of Psalm 119:30 calls the Way of Truth the Way of Faithfulness. In Hebrew, this phrase paints a picture of someone firmly gripping a plow as it pulls them forward.

It makes me think of water skiing. When trying to get up on your skis, you hold on to a rope attached to a boat. You must clutch the handle tightly to be pulled on top of the waves. When we treat faithfulness like that handlebar, gripping it with all our might, God will pull us up and forward, above anything trying to take us under. But to *stay* up, we must remain fully committed, no matter how rough the waters.

Jesus confirms this in Matthew 24. After listing all the characteristics of the end-time sway, He encourages us with these words: "But the one who endures to the end will be saved" (Matthew 24:13 ESV). This is a call to us all! No matter our age or stage of life, every one of us will one day reach the end of our time on earth, whether by death or Jesus' return. We will be saved only when we remain faithful—enduring on the Way to the end.

Unfortunately, faithfulness is not a widely cherished concept in our culture today. Instead, it seems like an epidemic of unfaithfulness has plagued us and threatened to take us under. As we've established, disciplines like attending church, tithing, and sanctity in marriage are no longer prized. Unfaithfulness hurts marriages, destroys families, and threatens the church of the living God. When we live with one grip here and one there, we live like children, "...tossed to and fro by the waves and carried about with every wind of doctrine" (Ephesians 4:14).

But God is not confused. His way is and always has been the Way of Faithfulness. His mindset will always be one of the covenant. "This is how one should regard us, as servants of Christ and stewards of the mysteries of God. Moreover, it is required of stewards that they be found faithful" (1 Corinthians 4:1-2 ESV).

This covenant mindset is why Jesus says, "No one, having put his hand to the plow, and looking back, is fit for the kingdom of God" (Luke 9:62). To remain on the Way to the end, we must keep our focus forward. There's no room for the lukewarm living of Laodecia. We can't be half in and half out.

THE YOU AFFECTS THE WE

Scripture shows that God's people, the Israelites, struggled with holding their grip. Their cycle of unfaithfulness kept them from His purposes for a long time. At one point in their nation's history, Babylon took them captive because of it.

"So all Israel was recorded by genealogies, and indeed, they were inscribed in the book of the kings of Israel. But Judah was carried away captive to Babylon because of their unfaithfulness" (1 Chronicles 9:1). The King James version calls it their *transgression*. It was a transgression—a *travesty*—of unfaithfulness. Eventually, as God promised, He delivered the Israelites from captivity and led them to the promised land, but because of their constant wavering, the journey took forty years.

When the Israelites finally entered the promised land, they encountered their first battle at Jericho. Jericho was a strong, secluded city with high and thick walls, but God instructed Israel's leader, Joshua, to overtake it. He also instructed him how. When the Israelites followed God's instructions, the walls of Jericho fell, and they claimed the city. Because Jericho was the first city the Israelites claimed in the promised land, God commanded them to treat it as a tithe, not taking any spoils with them. Instead, the treasures were to be reserved for God's house.

But you, keep yourselves from the things devoted to destruction, lest when you have devoted them, you take any of the devoted things and make the camp of Israel a thing for destruction and bring trouble upon it. But all silver and gold, and every vessel of bronze and iron, are holy to the Lord; they shall go into the treasury of the Lord (Joshua 6:18-19 ESV).

After leaving Jericho, the Israelites encountered the city of Ai. It was the next city to overtake, and it didn't look like a tough battle. It seemed like such an easy win that Joshua only sent 3,000 men to fight. Imagine his surprise when, after defeating the powerful city of Jericho, they *lost* to Ai!

Any kind of loss is disheartening, but this one was especially so. Joshua asked God why He had not been with them, and God explained why—"Israel has sinned; they have transgressed my covenant that I commanded them; they have taken some of the devoted things; they have stolen and lied and put them among their own belongings" (Joshua 7:11 ESV).

So Joshua called a big family meeting. He commanded all of Israel to come out of their tents and stand with their households so that God could show them who had taken the spoils. He identified Achan from the tribe of Judah as the perpetrator, so Joshua quickly dealt with that sin as God instructed. Once he did, God's favor returned, and Israel went back to Ai and defeated it. This story is a great lesson in faithfulness. Sins may appear small and hidden initially, but if they're not dealt with, they can completely demolish our homes.

You are the gatekeeper of your home, so what are you allowing into it? Who do you allow access to your family? Be careful with what tempts you to be unfaithful because what affects you *will* affect your household. And as we see from the story of Achan, what affects your house will ultimately affect God's house, too. The *you* always affects the *we*.

REBUILDING FROM RUBBISH

I can hear some of your thoughts now. *Matthew, I know that now, but I've already messed up. I've already hurt my family too badly and hurt God's kingdom more than I've helped it. There's no hope.* If that's you, I want to encourage you with another story of the people of Israel. It's found in the Book of Nehemiah.

At this point in the nation's history, Israel had again been taken captive, but this time, by Babylon. While in exile, Nehemiah, a Jew and top official in the Persian court, discovered that Jerusalem's walls had

> "The *you* always affects the *we*."

been destroyed. It troubled him deeply, and he was determined to rebuild the walls. With the king's favor, he and a group of Israelites returned to Jerusalem.

The Jews, known as "Judah," made this significant

complaint concerning the condition of the walls. "The strength of the laborers is failing, and there is so much rubbish that we are not able to build the wall" (Nehemiah 4:10). But Nehemiah led the Israelites with strength and faith through many adversities. They pushed through the rubbish and rebuilt the wall, completing the massive project in only 52 days.

If you feel there's too much rubbish in your life or situation, take heart! Just as the Israelites pushed through and built something great, God will give you the strength and grace to rebuild. God is a redeemer and a restorer. Nothing is too hard for Him.

My favorite part of the story occurred just before the rebuilding began—when Nehemiah gathered the people to instruct and encourage them. Now, consider the crowd of people he was speaking to. They had traveled all the way from Babylon, their exiled city, to their beloved homeland. Upon arrival, they found it completely destroyed. I'm sure their hearts were broken. But in those moments of deep despair, Nehemiah gave a powerful address that transcends time and circumstance.

> And I looked and arose and said to the nobles and to the officials and to the rest of the people, "Do not be afraid of them. Remember the Lord, who is great and awesome, and fight for your brothers, your sons, your daughters, your wives, and your homes" (Nehemiah 4:14 ESV).

Read the words of Nehemiah as though he is delivering them to you today! No matter what your situation looks like, what's right is worth the fight.

Your soul is worth it.

Your marriage is worth it.

Your family is worth it.

The enemy may be on a rampage, and our faithfulness might be under fire. But amid the rubbish, it's time to rise and say, "I'll fight for what matters!"

It won't be easy, just like it wasn't easy for the Israelites. It's never easy to go against the tide, pushing back on years of generational issues, but faithfulness is the only way to rebuild. Faithfulness is the only way to rise above the waters trying to take us under. Yes, walking God's way will inconvenience you. It's called the good *fight* of faith for a reason. But if it's right in God, then it's worth it.

> "What's right is worth the fight."

THE SEARCH IS ON

When speaking of culture's current state of unfaithfulness, it's important to note that *every* generation has had similar issues. People have *always* had a hard time with commitment, but God has *always* redeemed their mistakes. Without fail, Scripture proves God gives a unique blessing to those who do the work. The search is on for the faithful! And these two verses unveil the pursuit:

"For the eyes of the Lord range throughout the earth to strengthen those whose hearts are fully committed to him" (2 Chronicles 16:9).

"Many a man proclaims his own steadfast love, but a faithful man who can find?" (Proverbs 20:6 ESV).

In a world of ever-changing seasons, we can't be fair-weather Christians. We've got to be like Teflon—no matter our condition, we don't change. We *always* pray, we *always* praise, and we *always* endure hardships as soldiers of Christ because we're blood-bought believers in this for the long haul. Our faithfulness is the seed God needs to grow great

"The breakthrough is in the follow through!"

things on the earth, so stay with God. "I'm sure now I'll see God's goodness in the exuberant earth. Stay with God! Take heart. Don't quit! I'll say it again: Stay with God" (Psalm 27:13-14 MSG).

WHAT YOU DO AFTER

I realize it's easy to get pumped up reading about how God wants to bless us, but unless we take action, we'll never get to that place. Your advancement doesn't lie in a moment of inspiration; it relies on what you do after. I have said it for years: the breakthrough is in the follow-through!

Think of teenagers at church summer camp, in an environment charged with the presence of God. It's easy for them to get inspired. While there, they may surrender their lives to Him, resolving to remain faithful to His way. Though this passion is great, it doesn't sustain them. Many times, after returning home, their immaturity allows them to fall into their old routine. Within a few months, they're often right back where they started. Why does this happen? It is because they lacked follow-through. It's the continual work of the Word that brings true, lasting change. It is always about what you do *after*.

What do you do after a fall? You get back up.

What do you do after a victory? You stay humble.

What do you do after a loss? You seek wisdom.

What do you do after inspiration? You follow through.

To endure to the end of the Way, we've got to live in a continual state of follow-through. So now, let's talk about how.

FAITH-FULL-NESS

The first key to following through is that we aren't just faithful but faith-*full*, which means we are so convinced of God's purposes that we can't *help* but follow through.

I'd imagine that most of us respect the sovereignty of God. We believe He *can* do whatever He sets out to do. Our problem lies in believing that He *will*. Unbelief is one of the biggest strategies of the enemy. It's how he manipulated the very first sin in the world! He asked Eve, "Did God really say that?" God will do nothing until we first believe.

In John 20, after Jesus rose from the dead, He appeared to the disciples. One of them, Thomas, was not there when He appeared. After the other disciples told him what had happened, Thomas responded in verse 25, "I won't believe it unless I see the nail wounds in his hands, put my fingers into them, and place my hand into the wound in his side" (NLT).

"A natural faith believes because we see. A supernatural faith believes before we see."

Eight days later, Jesus appeared to the disciples again. This time, Thomas was there. He saw and touched Jesus' wounds, and he believed. In verse 29, Jesus tells Thomas, "You believe because you have seen me. Blessed are those who believe without seeing me." A natural faith believes *because* we see. A supernatural faith believes *before* we see. We are called to embrace the latter.

Do you *really* believe God wants to be good to you? Do you *really* believe He can heal your family? Your body? Your situation? Do you *really* believe He has a plan for your life? We will never remain faithful until we are first *faith-full*.

KEEP YOUR SOUL

Another key to staying faithful is keeping our souls healthy through the power of forgiveness. Our freedom relies on both accepting God's forgiveness and forgiving others. *Christ's* forgiveness set us free. *Our* forgiveness keeps us free.

This proverb is a good reminder of the damage unforgiveness can bring: "Like a dog that returns to his vomit is a fool who repeats his folly" (Proverbs 26:11 ESV). When we choose the "comfort" of unforgiveness over the discomfort of forgiveness, we stay stuck, but when we choose forgiveness, we're set free.

Along their journey on the Way, Israel valued comfort over truth. That's why they often wanted to return to captivity in Egypt after leaving it for the promised land. They wanted to go back to bondage because it was comfortable. But truly free people don't go back; they move forward into continued freedom. When

> *"Christ's* forgiveness set us free. *Our* forgiveness keeps us free."

we make a habit of giving and receiving forgiveness, we live in a continual state of freedom, and it's this freedom that helps us to remain faithful.

IT'S MORE ABOUT WHAT IS THAN WHAT'S NOT

One of the best ways to choose faithfulness is through contentment—working with what we have instead of wishing for what we don't have. That's because it's always more about what is than what's not. In a culture of constant comparison, seeing this can be difficult, but if we want to stay faithful to the end, it is also necessary.

We see a wonderful example of contentment in the story of John the Baptist. John's purpose was to prepare Israel for Jesus' coming. When Jesus finally came, John's followers started

> "Truly free people don't go back; they move forward into continued freedom."

following Jesus. John could have played the comparison game, but he didn't. Why? Because he was content with his purpose. This is evident in John 3:26 when John's followers brought up that many of his followers were now following Jesus. John the Baptist responded in verse 27 with, "A man can receive nothing unless it has been given to him from heaven."

Here is reality: none of us have it all. So, we can focus on what we don't have, living miserably, or we can focus on what we do have and live in contentment. Why does the enemy hit us so hard in this area? Because he knows that if he can take your contentment, he can take your vision. And without vision, you're stuck. In quitting comparison, remember that God will never hold you accountable for the talents, relationships, and circumstances you *don't* have. He'll only hold you responsible for what you *do* have.

And here is my judgment about what is best for you in this matter. Last year you were the first not only to give but also to have the desire to do so. Now finish the work, so that your eager willingness to do it may be matched by your completion of it, according to your means. For if the willingness is there, the gift is acceptable according to what one has, not according to what one does not have (2 Corinthians 8:10-12 NIV).

So what if you settled your season right now? What if you quit focusing on everything that wasn't? Everything that could have been? What if you looked at your marriage, kids, home, job, friends, church, and life and thought, "This is special." What if you found contentment in what is and gave no thought to what isn't?

> "It's always more about what is than what's not."

I've learned from experience—how you see it is how you'll treat it. So, I encourage you to take an inventory of your life today. See what God has given *you* and then determine to embrace it.

Celebrate it.

Prioritize it.

Thank God for it.

This will keep you on the Way to Faithfulness.

GIVE GOD TIME

Another key to faithfulness is patience—giving God time. In the process of seed, time, and harvest, it is our part to nurture the *seed*, and God's part happens in *time*. It's only when we honor both that the harvest comes.

Let's clarify: God doesn't ask for more time because He needs it. He's all-powerful. God asks for more time because He knows every detail of our situation. He knows every piece of our hearts and every plan for our future. And He wants to work in a way that not only helps us *today* but also transforms us, blessing our future and the futures of generations to come.

Time has always been the hardest part of the process for me. Just before the pandemic hit, our church was experiencing a season of stagnation. I was frustrated by the lack of progress and had started to believe that maybe I was the problem.

While driving our kids to school, I asked God what to do. My Bible app was reading Scripture to me in the background, and minutes later, the voice read Luke

"How you see it is how you'll treat it."

13:6-9—the Parable of the Barren Fig Tree. In this parable, a master sees a fig tree in his vineyard not bearing fruit, so he brings it up to the vinedresser.

Verses 7-9 ESV says, "'Look, for three years now I have come seeking fruit on this fig tree, and I find none. Cut it down. Why should it use up the ground?' The vinedresser replies, 'Sir, let it alone this year also until I dig around it and put on manure. Then if it should bear fruit next year, well and good; but if not, you can cut it down.'"

I knew what God was telling me: "Matthew, just give me a little more time."

Sometimes, things just take longer. Sometimes, they take more time, prayer, persistence, and faith. So if Jesus has given you a promise and you're contending for a breakthrough, give God time. Though the vision tarry, wait for it, knowing you *can* trust His process. As Psalm 27:13 says, you *will* see His goodness in the land of the living, but you've got to have a long faith. You've got to have faith that waits.

We see the importance of long faith in the story of Peter walking on water in Matthew 14:22-33. When Jesus called Peter out of the boat, he obeyed and stood on the water. Peter had faith, but it only lasted for a moment. As soon as he looked at the waves, he lost his confidence. He began sinking, crying out for Jesus to save him. His faith wasn't long enough.

Hebrews 6:12 tells us long faith requires two things—faith and patience: "... imitate those who through *faith* and *patience* inherit what has been promised" (Hebrews 6:12 NIV). When advancing on the Way, faith is like one leg and patience like the other. It takes both to keep walking. It takes both to remain faithful.

Have patience, have patience
Don't be in such a hurry
When you get impatient, you only start to worry
Remember, remember that God is patient, too

*And think of all the times when others have to wait
for you (The Music Machine).*[19]

ENDURE

The last key to breakthrough might be obvious, but
that doesn't mean it's easy. To remain faithful until the
end, we must do what Matthew 24:13 says and *endure*, no
matter what.

I know you're likely tired. I know the pressure is
mounting. Maybe once you felt strong, but that was
before life got heavy. Now, you feel you're barely moving. Scripture tells us what to do in moments like this.
A major key to endurance is trust—relying upon God's
strength above all else. "Therefore strengthen the hands
which hang down, and the feeble knees, and make
straight paths for your feet, so that what is lame may not
be dislocated, but rather be healed" (Hebrews 12:12-13).

When we're tempted to fear, we must assure ourselves that God will come to our aid, avenge us of our
spiritual enemies, and reward our efforts to serve Him.
"Say to those *who are* fearful-hearted, 'Be strong, do not
fear! Behold, your God will come *with* vengeance, *With*
the recompense of God; He will come and save you'"
(Isaiah 35:4). So when you feel weary, cry out to your Father. He *will* strengthen you.

As you endeavor to remain faithful to the end, I pray
that you follow through and fight for what is right. I

pray you embrace faith, forgiveness, contentment, patience, and trust with a renewed passion, knowing that God's not asking for perfection. He's just asking for a willing heart. If we will do our part, He will help us remain faithful—to the end.

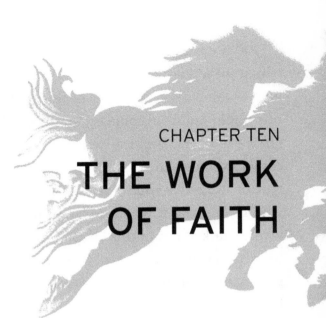

CHAPTER TEN
THE WORK OF FAITH

WELL, **WE'VE MADE** it to the end of our time together, and we've learned much on our journey. We've discerned the hour we live in and decided to walk the Way of Truth. Then, we applied the truth and started walking. Now, we're learning to abide—to remain faithful to the end. Paul called this process "the work of faith."

> "We give thanks to God always for all of you, constantly mentioning you in our prayers, remembering before our God and Father your work of faith and labor of love and steadfastness of hope in our Lord Jesus Christ" (1 Thessalonians 1:2-3 ESV).

As we embrace the work of faith, we'll build a life for which we're eternally grateful. On the journey, it will help to remember two types of stories. First, we should remember our testimonies, gratefully reflecting on how far we've come, because remembering how far we've come gives us the strength to go farther. The second type of stories we should remember are stories of those who have made it where we want to be. That's what I want to talk about in this chapter. In our last moments together, I want to give you an example of someone who successfully embraced the work of faith, remaining faithful to the end.

You probably know him as the original leader of God's people—Moses. Before we talk through his story, it's important to note this: Moses' life was not perfect, and neither was he. He faced many challenges and did not always respond to them in the right way. But God didn't give up on Moses, and Moses didn't give up on God. As Moses continually engaged in the work of faith, he proved himself faithful. We find the story of Moses and his great faith in the book of Hebrews.

> By faith Moses, when he became of age, refused to be called the son of Pharaoh's daughter, choosing rather to suffer affliction with the people of God than to enjoy the passing pleasures of sin, esteeming the reproach of Christ greater riches than the treasures in Egypt; for he looked to the

reward. By faith he forsook Egypt, not fearing the wrath of the king; for he endured as seeing Him who is invisible. By faith he kept the Passover and the sprinkling of blood, lest he who destroyed the firstborn should touch them. By faith they passed through the Red Sea as by dry land, whereas the Egyptians, attempting to do so, were drowned (Hebrews 11:24-29).

This passage might be short, but it paints a beautiful picture. Look closely, and you will find six profound actions Moses took that kept him on the Way of Faithfulness.

REFUSE

The first thing Moses did was refuse. Verse 24— "By faith Moses, when he became of age, *refused* to be called the son of Pharaoh's daughter."

To be faithful, you must always refuse something. You'll have to refuse to be labeled by your past. You'll have to refuse to operate as a victim of your circumstances. You'll have to refuse temptation, discouragement, defeat, offense, doubt, guilt, shame, mediocrity, apathy, and so much more.

CHOOSE

We don't stop at refusal, though. We refuse one thing so that we can choose another. That's what verse 25 shows us—"...*choosing* rather to suffer affliction with the people of God than to enjoy the passing pleasures of sin."

Moses refused the comfort of his past as royalty in Egypt so that he could choose God's plans for his future. The process is the same for us. When we refuse to sin, we can choose godliness. When we refuse to fear, we can choose faith. When we refuse our past, we can choose God's plans for our future. So don't short-sight your decisions. Remember that once you refuse, then you can choose. And what you choose can affect generations for eternity.

ESTEEM

The next choice Moses made was to esteem. Verse 26— "...*esteeming* the reproach of Christ greater riches than the treasures in Egypt; for he looked to the reward." When we esteem something, we cherish it, and what we cherish, we protect.

Moses proved by his actions that he esteemed God above all else. Moses was a prince in Egypt. He had everything he could ever need or want there, but he esteemed God and His purposes for his life—as challenging as they were—much more than any treasures. Because of that, he cherished and protected God's purposes. We too must esteem God and His approval over anyone else's. We have to esteem His purposes, His presence, and His purity. We've got to esteem His Word and His church. When we put Him first, He will take care of us, just as He did Moses.

Abby and I experienced the reality of this truth when we had just graduated from Bible school. We had worked hard to save a down payment for an apartment for our young family. We stashed every piece of spare change and loose bill in a Wells Fargo box underneath our bed.

We had about $400 out of the $1,200 we needed when we went to church one Sunday evening. In that service, a missionary was speaking. While he was talking, Abby leaned over to me and said, "Babe, I really feel we are supposed to give that $400 to his work." Honestly, I was reluctant because we had worked so hard for that money, and I knew time was ticking for us to save up the rest. However, I figured I should at least pray about it. When I did, I knew she was right, so we gave our entire savings in that service.

Two days later, my grandmother called me and said, "Matthew, I want to buy your family a small home. I'll put your name on the loan, and you can pay me $500 monthly toward the mortgage." I was floored. When we esteem God's work, He truly takes care of *everything* else.

FORSAKE

Forsaking was the next step Moses took. Verse 27— "By faith he *forsook* Egypt, not fearing the wrath of the king; for he endured as seeing Him who is invisible."

To follow Jesus, we too will have to forsake some

things. That's why Paul says in Philippians 3:13 ESV, "Brothers, I do not consider that I have made it my own. But one thing I do: forgetting what lies behind and straining forward to what lies ahead...." We cannot have the best of both worlds; it's either *all* of Jesus or *all* of the world. If we forsake the parts of our past that don't align with God's way, then, like Moses, we will endure.

KEEP

Another vital action Moses took was keeping. Verse 28—"By faith, he *kept* the Passover and the sprinkling of blood, lest he who destroyed the firstborn should touch them."

I see this key as having two parts. First, Moses kept the right priorities by keeping the Passover because it was holy. Throughout his life, he worked hard to keep God's instructions. When he messed up, he always did his best to get back on track. The second way Moses "kept" is by keeping on with patience. Patience is a commitment to faith beyond emotion. If we embrace the work of faith with patient endurance, we will persevere.

PASS

Now we enter the final breakthrough. Verse 29—"By faith, they *passed* through the Red Sea as by dry land, whereas the Egyptians, attempting to do so, were drowned."

This last key might not be something you would expect, but it's vital to enduring. To endure, we must pass through striving into a place of rest. When Moses approached the Red Sea with the Egyptians behind them, I'm sure he felt the pressure. I'm sure he was afraid and wondered if God would come through.

Moses had to push through fear and trust that if God said He would take care of them, He would. When he acted from that place of rest and trust, God saved the Israelites.

> "Patience is a commitment to faith beyond emotion."

It is the same for us. Every day, we must choose to place our lives in God's hands and walk in confidence in His sovereignty.

This is why Jesus said: "Come to me, all who labor and are heavy laden, and I will give you rest" (Matthew 11:28 ESV). It's also why Peter wrote: "Cast all your anxiety on him because he cares for you" (1 Peter 5:7 NIV). If we pass through anxiety and enter the rest of trust, we will make it to the end of God's glorious path, enjoying the journey along the way.

FAITH, HOPE, AND LOVE

Before we conclude our time together, I want to encourage you with one more thing. Ecclesiastes 4:12 NLT says, "...a triple-braided cord is not easily broken." You have probably heard this referencing a Christ-centered marriage. There's another cord that's not easily broken, though, and we find it in 1 Corinthians 13:13 NIV. It says,

"And now these three remain: faith, hope and love. But the greatest of these is love."

As we continue in the work of faith, we must not forget about the other two parts of the cord. The second strand—hope—is vital to keeping our spirits strong. We do this by continually praising God for what He's doing: "...let us continually offer up a sacrifice of praise to God..." (Hebrews 13:15 ESV). The author calls it a "sacrifice of praise" because, often, that's how it feels. We don't always *feel* like praising, but remembering all God has done in the past stirs up our hope that He can do it again.

This is why Jude 1:21 ESV says, "keep yourselves in the love of God..." When we keep ourselves in Christ's love and extend that love to others, it strengthens our hope and faith, allowing us to continue on The Way.

Friend, I am *so* glad you've chosen The Way. I'm grateful you've wisely chosen to love God above all else. I believe in your ability to resist the enemy's detours and faithfully continue on The Way of Truth. I know you will honor the Place of Truth, and I know you will listen for the Guide and follow the Map, sowing in faith and enjoying the fruit along the way.

I hope we cross paths again, but if not, know I am cheering you on. And when we both finish our journey, I'll see you at the end.

CONNECT:

Instagram:
@matthewpollock1

Twitter:
@matthewpollock1

Facebook:
@PastorMatthewPollock

Website:
www.thewayfamilychurch.com

Church Address:
38710 Sky Canyon Dr, Murrieta, CA 92563

Email:
info@matthewpollock.org

MATTHEW POLLOCK is a gifted speaker and dynamic leader, passionate about building the local church and helping people engage in a genuine relationship with God. In 2008, Matthew and his wife Abby began The Way Family Church in Murrieta, California—a spirit-filled church that exists to reach the area with the message of Jesus. Matthew and Abby have been married for 21 years. They have four children—Talon, Kaleb, Hope, and Brooke—and one daughter-in-law, Ariana.

APPENDIX:
A PRAYER FOR SALVATION

If you're ready to accept Jesus as Lord and Savior of your life—choosing the Way once and for all—pray this prayer with me:

Jesus,

Thank you for your invaluable gift of salvation. Today, I accept that gift. I repent of my sins and renounce my past. I believe in my heart and confess with my mouth that you are the seed of salvation. From today on, I ask you to live inside of me. Holy Spirit, make your home in my heart. Plant me in your church. Help me walk in the principles of your Word. Use me for your glory and give me a growing love for the Way.

In your name, I pray, Amen.

Congratulations! You just made the most important decision you'll ever make. You're now walking the Way! I know this all might be new to you, and you might have questions or need help to figure out what's next. If that's the case, or if you'd like to talk with someone about your decision, we are here to help. Email us at info@ thewayfamilychurch.com, and we'll assist you in getting started. Welcome to the family of God!

ENDNOTES

1. Dallas, Kelsey. "The State of Faith." Deseret News, March 22, 2022. https://www.deseret.com/faith/2022/3/21/22981634/the-state-of-faith-american-religion-research-marist-poll.

2. "American Worldview Inventory 2021 Release #3." Arizona Christian University Cultural Research Center. Accessed November 13, 2022. https://www.arizonachristian.edu/wp-content/uploads/2021/05/CRC_AWVI2021_Release03_Digital_01_20210512.pdf.

3. Bernis, Jonathan. "How Many Prophecies Did Jesus Fulfill?" FIRM Israel, May 24, 2022. https://firmisrael.org/learn/how-many-prophecies-did-jesus-fulfill/.

4. "One in Three Practicing Christians Has Stopped Attending Church during COVID-19." Barna Group. July 8, 2020. https://www.barna.com/research/new-sunday-morning-part-2/.

5. "One in Three Practicing Christians Has Stopped Attending Church."

6. "Who We Are." Chick-fil-A. Accessed November 12, 2022. https://www.chick-fil-a.com/about/who-we-are.

7. Taylor, Kate. "Chick-Fil-A Likely Loses out on More than $1 Billion in Sales Every Year by Closing on Sundays - and It's a Brilliant Business Strategy." Business Insider. July 29, 2019. https://www.businessinsider.com/chick-fil-a-closes-on-sunday-why-2019-7.

8. Lea, Brittany De. "This Is How Much the Average Chick-Fil-A Made in 2020." Fox Business. July 26, 2021. https://www.foxbusiness.com/retail/how-much-average-chick-fil-a-made-2020.

9. Maldre, Matt. "John 16:33 Overcome = Nenikēka." Christian notebook. August 22, 2021. https://christiannotebook.com/john-16v33-overcome-nenikeka/.

10. Barnes Notes, https://biblehub.com/commentaries/1_timothy/4-1.htm, (Accessed December 11, 2022).

11. https://www.bibletools.org/index.cfm/fuseaction/Lexicon.show/ID/G4490/rhetos.htm (Accessed December 11, 2022).

12. https://kingjamesbibledictionary.com/Dictionary/Anathema (Accessed December 13, 2022).

13. https://biblehub.com/hebrew/7337.htm (Accessed December 13, 2022).

14. https://biblehub.com/greek/1465.htm (Accessed November 22, 2022).

15. https://www.britannica.com/topic/Ecclesia-ancient-Greek-assembly (Accessed November 22, 2022).

16. https://www.spurgeon.org/resource-library/sermons/recruits-for-king-jesus/#flipbook/ (Accessed December 15, 2022).

17. https://www.americanrhetoric.com/speeches/bononationalprayerbreakfast.htm (Accessed November 13, 2022).

18. Robert Jamieson, https://www.preceptaustin.org/hebrews_1024-25 (Accessed December 16, 2022).

19. http://www.hisandhernandezmusic.com/store/Details.cfm?ProdID=6544 (Accessed December 17, 2022).

For information on bulk orders, contact us at:
TALLPINEBOOKS.COM

Printed in the USA
CPSIA information can be obtained
at www.ICGtesting.com
LVHW092323020923
756224LV00003B/5/J